On Scottish Links

The Old Course 1st, 17th, and 18th

On Scottish Links

Photography **Iain Macfarlane Lowe**

& Christopher J. Lowe

Text **George Peper**

Kingsbarns 15th green from the 12th green

This edition is published by:
Iain Lowe Photography
10 Fergusson Place
St Andrews, Fife KY16 9NF
Scotland

Design by Savitski Design

Printed and bound in China

ISBN: 978-0-9571431-0-4

THE COURSES

THE OLD COURSE

THE HOME OF GOLF

THE OLD COURSE ✥ AN INTRODUCTION

When tennis is played in the Acropolis, when cricket balls carom through the pillars of Stonehenge, when basketball comes to the Sistine Chapel—only then will non-golfers begin to know what it's like to set foot on the Old Course at St Andrews. This is not a golf course, it is the sure and sacred crucible of man's best game.

The Old Lady, as she is known, is a woman of uncertain age. Her birthday—indeed her birth century—is lost in the mists of time, though no one disputes that she has been around for at least half a millennium. Equal uncertainty reigns with regard to her first suitors. They may have been Dutch traders, importing a game called colf across the North Sea. Or perhaps they were simply home-grown lads, shepherds using their wooden crooks to propel stones across the dunescape.

It doesn't matter, really. The compelling question is not how golf on the Old Course began but where we would all be if it hadn't. There would be no Tiger Woods. There would be no Pine Valley or Muirfield. No Masters. No Big Bertha. There would be no whiffs, shanks, gimmes, or holes-in-one. And fifty million of the world's citizens would be without a magnificent obsession.

So let us give thanks to those pilgrims, whoever they may have been, and thanks above all to Mother Nature for the splendid playground she provided. Oh, it may not have had much in the way of eye appeal; neither shimmering seaside nor wooded glen, it fell literally between them—linksland—a slender stretch of all but barren terrain, riddled with humps and troughs. As such, however, it was ideally suited to the propulsion and pursuit of a little white ball.

By the time anyone was counting, the Old Course had 22 holes, but before long the number was reduced to 18, with eight of the greens doing double duty for the outward and inward nines. Groups played toward the same putting cups, but from opposite directions.

As golf grew in popularity, however, this became untenable—indeed dangerous—and in 1832 the greens were enlarged to accommodate two separate cups. At the same time the fairways were widened—in fact, more than doubled in width—with the result that an important new element was introduced: strategy. No longer were players forced to follow a straight and narrow path. There was leeway, room to plot and pursue the most propitious path to the hole, depending on the prevailing conditions and one's own reserves of skill and courage. Thinking man's golf was born.

◄ It all starts here: book in with the starter, a practice putt and onto the first tee.

The Old Course coaxes and cajoles us, beckons our best golf and punishes our worst. It commands our attention and provokes our imagination, exhorts us to choose the right shot and then hit the right shot right. When we manage to do that—when our lofted 5-iron or punched wedge finds its way to the pin—we feel a satisfaction that the mere strike of club on ball can never produce.

No other course has had the knack of identifying not just champions, but the very best players of their eras. Bobby Jones, Jack Nicklaus, and Tiger Woods each have won two titles here. No other course has been such a living resource for golf course architects. From C.B. Macdonald and H.S. Colt through Alister Mackenzie, Donald Ross, and Albert Tillinghast to Robert Trent Jones, Pete Dye, and the current generation of minimalists—all of them have studied the Old Course and brought her lessons to bear in every corner of the world.

And surely no other course has brought so much pleasure to so many golfers of every stripe. The astonishing fact is that twice as much golf has been played on the Old Course as on any other course in the world—something very close to one billion strokes. One billion and counting, for the Old Lady has lost none of her charm.

A young Bobby Jones met his match here during the third round of the 1921 Open Championship, taking four strokes in Hill bunker (bottom right) before picking up his ball and walking off the course.

HOLE № 1 BURN

Were you to be transported magically to the first tee of the Old Course—not knowing what it is—you might reasonably deem it the perfect setting for any number of activities, none of them golf.

The two miles of broad sandy beach just to your right suggests a day of sunning or surfcasting. The flat green lawn unfurling in front of you could host a football match or even a few chukkers of polo. The gleaming white boundary fencing brings to mind the rails at Churchill Downs or Ascot. And the imposing, enclosing stone architecture—rife with spectators both real and imagined—suggests a latter day Colosseum.

But golf it is and the opening task, on the surface at least, couldn't be simpler—find a fairway that is 130 yards wide. This, however, is the Old Course, and to stand on this tee for the first time is to feel the weight of history, of all the shots that have preceded yours. You know you can hit the fairway—the question is whether you can hit the ball. So intimidating is this assignment that Dwight Eisenhower, a five-star general who once held the fate of the free world in his hands, couldn't pull the trigger. Instead he slinked quietly to the second hole.

Beyond the fear factor, this hole bares its fangs when the breeze blows. Into a stiff headwind its 376 yards can play more like 476—an all-carry 476, as the Swilken Burn runs across the front edge of the green. The 1976

U.S. Open Champion Jerry Pate recalls playing in a collegiate event where the wind was so strong that he hit a driver and 3-wood and was still short of the burn. When a crosswind blows from the southwest, as it often does, the right-hand out-of-bounds fence suddenly closes in and the same thing happens on the opposite side when the wind comes from off the sea.

Ironically, today's number one was the last hole added to the Old Course. When additional land became available in 1870 Old Tom Morris built a new green and re-routed the first fairway (up until that time, the hole had shared a green with number 17). Unwittingly that change—calling for a forced carry over water—presaged the "target golf" brand of architecture that would take hold decades later in America.

It's often said you could play the entire Old Course with a putter, were it not for this hole, the only one where the ball cannot be rolled onto the green (it must be lofted). Indeed, on this course where alternative routes and myriad choices are the keynote, one of the few strategic mandates is this: on the approach to the first green, take at least one club more than you think you need. Even if you overhit the shot, leaving a chip or long putt back to the hole, the worst score you're likely to begin with is a 5, whereas if your ball should plunge into the burn, the best score you're likely to make is a 5.

◄ Old Course
1st tee to green

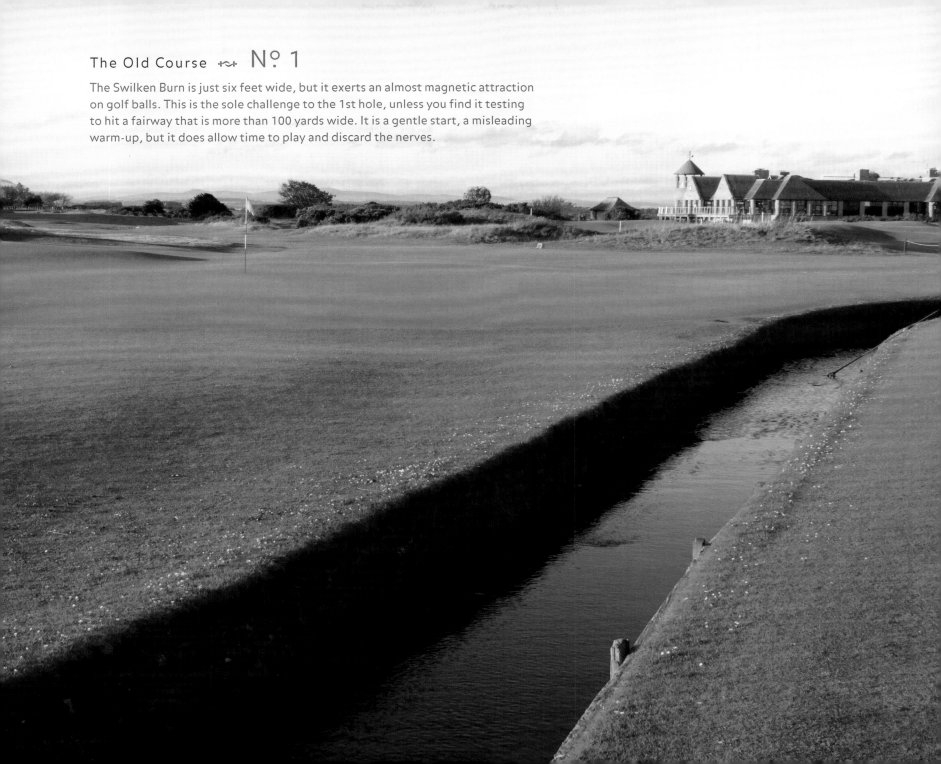

The Old Course ↭ Nº 1

The Swilken Burn is just six feet wide, but it exerts an almost magnetic attraction on golf balls. This is the sole challenge to the 1st hole, unless you find it testing to hit a fairway that is more than 100 yards wide. It is a gentle start, a misleading warm-up, but it does allow time to play and discard the nerves.

The Old Course ⤳ № 2

A savage section of gorse obscures the right side of
the fairway. Prudence suggest a wide berth to the left.

The right half of the green at the first hole melts seamlessly into the tee of the second—one continuous level expanse, all of it running at about the same speed on the Stimpmeter. And that is where all kinship between these two holes ends.

At number two, the course tacks forty-five degrees to the right, heading on the northward path it will maintain for the next six holes. If at the first hole the wind was in your face, it's now quartering from the left; if it blew from the left on number one, you probably didn't notice because the sturdy buildings of the Auld Grey Toon provide an excellent windbreak. Now, suddenly you feel it at your back.

Along with the switch of direction and shift in the wind comes a fundamental change in the character of the course. Whereas the opening hole was simple and straightforward, requiring little in the way of strategy, what begins now is a relentless examination in game management, a series of assignments calling for both careful thought and solid shotmaking. It is the second hole that sets the tone of the Old Course.

"Monotone", the critics might say, citing a sameness between this hole and the two that follow it. First-time players often have difficulty distinguishing among holes two, three, and four, in part because each of them begins with a semi-blind teeshot.

Indeed the most imposing sight from the second tee is the Old Course Hotel, the deluxe six-storey hostelry whose jutting façade was once likened by Henry Longhurst to "a dresser with its drawers pulled out." However, it is the other side that compels attention—a savage stretch of gorse obscures the right half of the fairway and runs the entire length of the hole, swallowing anything that strays its way.

Prudence suggests a wide berth to the left, but that brings its own set of perils. Shorter hitters risk the rough that separates this fairway from the 17th, while stronger players risk falling into the clutches of Cheape's Bunker, lurking invisibly, further up on the left edge of the fairway.

The choice here, as it will be so often on the Old Course, is whether to defy the hungry gorse and rough with an aggressive drive down the right side of the hole. The reward for those who succeed will be a far less vexing approach.

The first of the course's eight double greens is shared with the 16th hole (each pair of greens adds up to 18). The right side is unprotected and virtually flat but the left is a topographic carnival, with a ridge sweeping diagonally toward the higher area of the 16th and an assortment of humps and bowls menacing both the green and its entrance. When the pin is back-left, only a superbly executed shot will find it—those who fall short will have to pitch or putt through the rollercoaster.

A tee shot to the left side is the safer route but leaves a more challenging approach to the green. The aerial view clearly shows the vexing ridges on the left and the easier entry from the flatter right side, where the only concern is the claustrophobically bunkered 3rd tee.

The global golf landscape is full of tightly bunkered greens. This hole offers what has to be the world's most tightly bunkered tee. Four gaping pots surround the white markers, none of them more than a half dozen paces away. They belong not to this hole, but the previous one where, like many Old Course bunkers, they have become all but irrelevant, the quirky result of what happens when an ancient course must push back its tees in response to modern technology.

If the claustrophobia of sand leaves some players feeling a bit off balance, that's all right because this par four can be that kind of hole. On the scorecard it looks simple enough. At 370 yards, it's actually reachable downwind by power hitters whose drives bound fortunately across its humpy fairway. (This is true of nearly half the par fours on the Old Course. In a practice round for the 2000 Open Championship, Australian Scott Hend drove six of them.)

Distance is not the issue here, accuracy is, and as at the second hole, determining the line for one's teeshot is no simple matter. Once again gorse eclipses the view of the right side while a fescue-clad hillock is just tall enough to block the left. This is one hole where, before pulling the trigger, it's wise to consult either a caddie or a pin sheet. When the hole location is on the left—

especially the front-left—the wise strategy is to tack right. Otherwise the next shot will have to be played across a cavernous sand-filled crescent called Cartgate, six feet deep with a near-vertical front wall.

On the other hand, a drive that sails too far right will bring its own risk, with a parade of five pot bunkers ready to snare tee shots of all sizes. Even a strong and straight drive can leave a dodgy assignment, as a series of ridges and ripples cut across this fairway. Getting a level lie on this fairway is about as likely as getting a phone call from the queen.

A final complication is the last 70 yards of terrain before the green, where a sudden upward surge—literally a groundswell—occurs, hiding the putting surface and cautioning against a low-running approach while adding an extra frisson of trepidation to the alternative shot—the dreaded half wedge.

A slight tug and the ball will find Cartgate; a push and it could slip into swales on the right, a whisker heavy and it will never reach the green, and even the least bit thin and it will skitter across the billowing green to the rough beyond.

Indeed, the least stressful way to make par on this little hole may be to drive the green and three putt.

◄ 3rd tee to green

Approach from the left side and the cavernous
Cartgate bunker has to be cleared.

Four hundred and nineteen yards, twelve bunkers, half an acre of gorse and heather, and a menacing mound—that's what lies in wait on the par four named Ginger Beer. No wonder it was here that the early St Andrews golfers needed a drink.

For the world's best players this is the most difficult hole on the front nine and the second hardest on the course, exceeded only by famed number 17. Over the past seven Open Championships it has yielded a total of 201 birdies. By contrast, the par five that follows it gave up 211 birdies in 2005 alone. Although no statistics are available for amateurs, for most mortals on most days, par here is a cherished score.

Once again, the landing area is all but invisible from the tee. What you do see is a raised area of rough to the left and the ubiquitous border of gorse to the right. In the distance a pair of hillocks bulge from either side of the fairway, creating a narrow passageway through which the green is visible.

It is a hole that favours the long hitter. Anyone strong enough or blessed with a sufficient tailwind can clear the plateau on the left with nothing but fairway beyond—unless the ball should reach the 300-yard range, in which case it will trundle into Cottage, the third largest bunker on the course. To the right lurks a rich variety of trouble—along with the gorse are bunkers, heather, long grass, and a cart path.

◄ 4th tee view

On the way to the green, seven more pot bunkers await a missed shot. However, the feature that dominates the second shot is a large mound, smack in front of the green. Roughly five feet high and ten feet in diameter, it has the appearance of a sodded-over VW Beetle.

More often than not, the flagstick is positioned front and centre on this green and when that happens the mound plays first with golfers' minds and then with their shots. A severely short ball will pelt into the front slope and slide backward; a slightly long one will catch the downslope and shoot forward across the green; a shot that catches either side slope will be tossed comprehensively off line.

Salient natural features such as this mound constitute the unique and enduring challenge of the Old Course. The best of them occur within the last five or ten yards of the green, as a sort of goal-line stand by the Old Lady. Consider the burn at the first hole, the gauntlet of humps and hollows at the second, the hunchback ridge in front of the third. At virtually every hole a player must step back and decide just how to grapple with this fascinating last line of defence.

Everything about the 4th is challenging—the drive length and line, the humps, ridges, and bunkers on the approach, and the rippled putting surface. Par is a good score here.

The Old Course caddies have a mantra: "Left is right, right is shite." Nowhere is that advice more pertinent than on the tee of number five. In the rough to the starboard of this fairway are the Seven Sisters. Women of ill repute, all of them, they lure anyone with the slightest inclination to stray. To bounce among—but not into—these bunkers is to know what architect Alister Mackenzie referred to as "the pleasurable excitement of links golf."

Far safer is the left-hand route where the sole issue is an extended ridge that separates this hole from the higher terrain of hole 14. These are the only par fives on the course and their parallel position midway in their respective nines dramatizes one of the idiosyncratic charms of the Old Course: the hole sequences of the front and back nine are mirror images of each of other. In other words, if you fold the scorecard in the middle, the pars of the holes match up exactly—the two par threes (eight and 11) meet each other, as do five and 14, with all the other holes matching fours. It was all utterly unintended, and yet what other course in the world can make this claim?

A total of 15 bunkers await on this hole and the second shot must deal with the two most formidable—a pair known as the Spectacles—which bracket the fairway as it rises upward, roughly one hundred yards short of the green. The ideal line for the teeshot is the left-hand bunker. Back in the 1933 Open Championship, Craig Wood took dead aim and, aided by a strong tailwind and a rock hard fairway, actually reached the bunker, a record clout of 430 yards. Shortly thereafter the hole was lengthened by 46 yards. Still, in all but a headwind this 514-yard hole is reachable in two by both pros and amateurs.

Ah, but once again there is a final hurdle, a goal-line stand to be dealt with, this time in the form of a ten-foot-deep swale that protects the full width of the green entrance. A low, skittering shot may scoot happily down and up onto the green but a lofted ball that hits the upslope will return to the depths, leaving a blind pitch, chip or putt where distance control is a challenge.

Since the fairway rises up just before the swale, obscuring a view of the green, players often have no idea whether their approach shots have succeeded. One of the game's consummate joys is clambering hopefully up that final slope and finding one's ball within a short distance of the hole.

This green, shared with hole 13, is the largest on the course. At nearly 38,000 square feet, it could contain the first ten greens at Pebble Beach. If you were to hand mow it you'd have to walk nearly five miles. Happily, your only task is to hit a ball toward the hole, not a simple task either as the difference between a front and back pin placement on this behemoth can be 70 yards or more.

◄ Four of the drivable
Seven Sisters on 5th

The undulating 5th fairway and
Seven Sisters bunkers, right.

The eight-foot-deep gully protecting the front of the 5th green should be all that denies a birdie. And yet there is more. The sheer size of this green, where 60-foot putts are common, demands keen judgment and a sure stroke.

For certain players, this is the most terrifying teeshot on the course. We're referring to the trajectorially challenged—those who struggle to get their drives up in the air. The problem is a combination of what you can see and can't see. What you can't see is any part of the fairway. What you can see—directly in front of you—is what obscures it, a raised dune grown thick with heather and gorse, interrupted only by a narrow footpath. As you walk off this tee you feel as if you're heading on a nature walk.

To hurdle that area, you will need to hit a shot with a fair amount of both height and might. A 150-yard punch won't make it, particularly if there's any kind of wind. The rather mortifying alternative is to orient yourself ninety degrees counterclockwise, take a putter, and slap the ball across the 13th green, ideally to the narrow strip of fairway in front of the green. From there you'll have an unobstructed view—and an approach shot of 350 yards.

Just off this tee to the right is an elevated area—a sort of lookout point along the white shell road that parallels the first third of the course. Often, one of the pace-of-play rangers will park himself here and act as a forecaddie, signalling groups on the tee that the fairway is clear and they're free to hit. This spot would seem a perfect place to position a forward tee, or a ladies' tee. Much of the suffering would be alleviated—and with less time spent searching for topped tee shots, pace of play would improve as well. Why that has never been done is an enduring mystery.

But back to the assignment at hand. In the middle of the confronting thicket stands a white wooden directional pole. The general opinion among locals is that it induces players to aim a bit left of the actual centre of the fairway, but that's a good thing, as once again the thick gorse haunts the right side.

Any ball launched successfully over that pole will find a flat lie and a relatively uncomplicated shot to the green. Those who veer right or left, however, may hear their fellow players or caddies mutter the most dire of St Andrean words: "bunkerish," i.e. "I'm not positive, but that shot had the look of a ball headed toward a deep cavern of sand."

Six bunkers lie in the right rough with four more on the left including The Coffins, a pair of large and deep ones that also terrorize teeshots at the 13th hole. Also on that left side is a sizeable bed of heather for which the hole is named.

The last defence is once again a swale—not nearly as deep as the one at five but something to be factored in, especially since this green, although among the flattest on the course, slopes from front to back. Players tend to ponder this approach shot more than most, mulling whether to bump a low ball through the gully or try to stop a high one on the front of the green. Add a tail or headwind to the equation, and the quandary intensifies.

◄ View from the 6th tee

A sizeable bed of heather for
which the hole is named

Number seven marks the end of the journey northward and the beginning of the sequence of holes known as The Loop. The eighth and ninth holes double back to the south, then 10 and 11 return north to complete the circuit. A tacit ambition of any Old Course regular is to one-day play The Loop in five straight 3s. It isn't an impossible dream, especially under benign conditions, as two of the holes are par threes and two others are short and vulnerable fours. Without question, the toughest birdie is this one.

Once again—and for the last time—the line of sight is blocked on the right by gorse and sandhills, but visible three miles away, on the far bank of the Eden estuary, is the RAF Leuchars Air Station, home to several hundred servicemen and their jets. Under certain wind conditions, the airfield's tall white tower makes a perfect target for the tee shot. That is altogether fitting and proper because this hole itself occasionally requires the services of an air traffic controller: its fairway criss-crosses with that of number 11.

Power is once again a huge asset, as an abrupt ridge forms a wall across the fairway at about the 220-yard mark. Those who can fly it will bound forward into an open area with only a wedge to the green; those who fall short will tumble back into a divot-scarred valley, facing a blind shot with anything from a middle-iron to fairway wood.

If there is any good news for the latter group it is the fact that, as they settle over their approach shots, they will not be face-to-face with Shell, the second-largest bunker on the course. Three-quarters of an acre in area, it could comfortably accommodate a four-bedroom home with swimming pool and tennis court. The other good news for short hitters is that they're out of harm's way, while those with wedges in their hands stand smack in the path of teeshots fired from number 11.

For as long as anyone can remember, players teeing off 11 were allowed the right of way, in keeping with the "homeward-bound-players-first" policy that prevails everywhere (except at the first and 18th), where players teeing off on the back nine have the honour. Then a few years ago an experiment gave the honour to golfers playing number seven. That was quickly aborted and now good sense prevails—everyone keeps an eye on everyone else and the ballistic ballet more or less choreographs itself.

What awaits on the other side of Shell bunker is the widest and wildest double green on the course. Fully 112 yards from the left of the 11th to the right of the seventh, it spills downward through a series of pronounced ridges. Even those who approach with short irons should allow for some left-to-right drift if they want to secure the first of those five 3s.

◄ The view from the 7th tee is somewhat limited—the red 11th flag and Strath Bunker are really all you see.

The view of the approach
from a well-hit tee shot.

It was on the tee of this hole that Bobby Jones said he was paid the greatest compliment of his life. The year was 1936, and Jones was paying a casual visit to St Andrews as part of a European vacation. He had hoped to play a casual round on the Old Course, without any fanfare, but once word circulated among the St Andreans that their beloved Bobby was back, all the town's shops closed and most of the citizenry flooded to the course to watch him play.

Play he did, going to the turn in 33, including a 2 at the eighth. After he hit the tee shot that set up that birdie, his caddie, a young local lad, looked up at Jones with stars in his eyes and said, "My, sir, but you're a wonder."

Not much has changed at this hole since Jones's day—or for that matter since Old Tom Morris' day—except for the addition of a back tee that is seldom used. Between the tee and green is a stretch of broken ground, covered with fescue and heather, with a single pot bunker cut into a small hillside at the left front of the green. There is no fairway, no opportunity to bump and run onto this surface—and as such the strategic options are fewer than at any hole since the first. Essentially, you must fly the ball to the green.

The main issue can be wind direction, which is now the 180-degree opposite of what it was for the previous six holes—if you were riding a tailwind you now have a breeze in the face. The most challenging situation, however, is a downwind shot to a pin that is up front, as this green spills from front to back. A subtle ridge, just a few paces in front of the green further complicates the assignment.

The hole is 166 yards to the centre of the green. With a forward pin, it comes down to about 145. Since you won't be getting any backspin in that following wind—and the ball will bounce and roll after landing—you ideally need to land it about the 125-yard mark. The trouble with that is, there's almost nowhere to land the ball at the 125-yard mark—the pot bunker and the fronting ridge are there.

So you have two choices. The prudent one is to fly the ball onto the green, let it roll out, and accept a lengthy return putt. The other one—if for instance you're two down in a Nassau bet and you need to win this hole to avoid losing the front nine—is to try to loft as high a shot as possible onto the very front of the green, perhaps even a yard or two short of it (that's about all you have to work with) and hope that it releases down to the hole.

If that shot doesn't come off, you'll be chipping or flopping or blasting in the hope of saving par. If it does—if you succeed in leaving yourself a short putt for birdie—you'll be fully warranted in saying to yourself, "My, sir, but you're a wonder."

◄ The all-carry 8th

The most challenging situation, however,
is a downwind shot to a pin at the front.

It's likely that the best back-to-back shots ever struck in competition on the Old Course occurred in the first round of the 1921 Open Championship when Jock Hutchison holed his teeshot for an ace at number eight and then hit a drive at nine that likely would have gone into the hole had an overzealous spectator not raced onto the green and removed the flagstick. Instead, the ball hit the hole and stopped on the lip. Hutchison went on to win the title in a play-off over Roger Wethered.

This is a hole where even a middling golfer has a chance of making an eagle, and maybe even a hole in one. Just 289 yards from the regular tee (347 from the championship tee, which was not used in the 2005 Open), when it plays downwind it can be reached with a long iron. In truth, this is probably the easiest hole in championship golf.

For the first time since hole number one, the entire landing area is in plain view. At last there is no trouble to the right—just the returning 10th fairway. The encroaching row of gorse now looms on the left side, along with a double bunker named Kruger. Installed by Old Tom Morris at around the time of the Boer War, it is named after Paul Kruger, then president of the Transvaal. A second bunker, Mrs. Kruger, lies in the left rough about 50 yards ahead.

Today, neither Kruger comes into play except in an extremely strong headwind or after a cold-topped teeshot. However, two others do. The Boase's and End

Hole bunkers are demonically positioned in the centre of the fairway at 195 and 223 yards, respectively. Without them, this hole, with the flattest fairway on the course, would resemble a massive putting green.

In the 2000 Open Championship, Tiger Woods famously avoided all 112 of the Old Course bunkers for four days. On this hole, while his competitors gunned for the green with drivers, he chose a short iron, laid up short of the bunkers and then pitched onto the green, making three birdies and a par.

One final bunker—not much bigger than a bathtub—lurks at the front-left of the green. For years, it hid unnoticed under the branches of a gorse bush, but for the 2010 Open Championship the bush was pared back and the bunker deepened, in hopes of catching a teeshot or two from the world's best.

The second of the single greens on the course, this is also the flattest one in St Andrews. There is a good deal of room behind it, however, so the hole could easily be lengthened and made more challenging and interesting. It's unlikely though, that a change of that magnitude will ever be made on the Old Course.

Besides, there's something to be said for an easy ninth hole. A beacon of hope to the golfer who has struggled through the outward holes, it offers the possibility of a restorative birdie, a bit of psychological girding before the returning battle to the clubhouse.

◄ The 9th fairway in full view

For the first time in the round, the left side
of the fairway is the place to be. Once the
bunkers are escaped this becomes a chance
for birdie, or even better for the big hitters.

From late spring through to early autumn a small truck stations itself fifty yards or so behind the ninth green. When its side panel is lifted it becomes a refreshment stand that offers an array of hot and cold items to eat and drink.

During the cold months, however, the intrepid Old Course golfers are on their own. And so it is that at this tee, many of them pause for a moment and reach into their bags for a bit of sustenance—a candy bar perhaps, or on the most bone-chilling days a soothing nip of Scotland's other gift to the world.

No matter the season or choice of tonic, a bit of invigoration is wise before setting forth on the inward nine, for this is by unanimous agreement the more difficult of the two—a bit longer and a lot tighter, with out-of-bounds beckoning on four of the last five holes.

Indeed, it may be argued that the only hole on the second nine without some element of snarling intimidation is number 10. Side by side with the ninth, it plays across the same flat terrain and is only a few yards longer. It is curious that these are the two most pedestrian holes on the course. Maybe the founding shepherd had second thoughts about his routing and said, "Let's make this loop quick and simple so we can right the path and head back to town."

On days when the ninth hole is not drivable in one because of a strong wind, the tenth is. Three bunkers hide in the rough to the left, but they're barely 100 yards off the tee, so only the worst of drives will find them. Yes, there is heather and gorse over there but the heather is actually more help than hindrance—just dense enough to slow down a ball headed for the gorse, but generally not thick enough to snag a clubface.

A drive that skitters across the ninth fairway may visit one of the Krugers, but the main bunker to be dealt with here is a large and enveloping one on the right at the 250 mark, with another hiding just beyond it. For those who can hit a low, running draw this is the place to summon it, aiming at the left edge of the first bunker, and riding the firm, fast fairway toward the green.

The green is slightly raised but a swale collects anything short and right. Ask a local what the key is on this hole and he'll tell you it's getting the second shot all the way back to the pin. Maybe it's the fact that this is the second-largest green on the course, over fifty yards in depth. Maybe the frontal contours of the green make club selection difficult, maybe it's just that golfers chronically underclub. Whatever the reason, it's ironic that players typically need three shots to reach pin high on this rather short hole.

◄ The only hole on the second nine without some element of snarling intimidation is number 10.

The intimidating gorse and heather on the left force many teeshots to the right where the bunkers come into play. On the scorecard this looks like a birdie hole, but it's deceptively difficult.

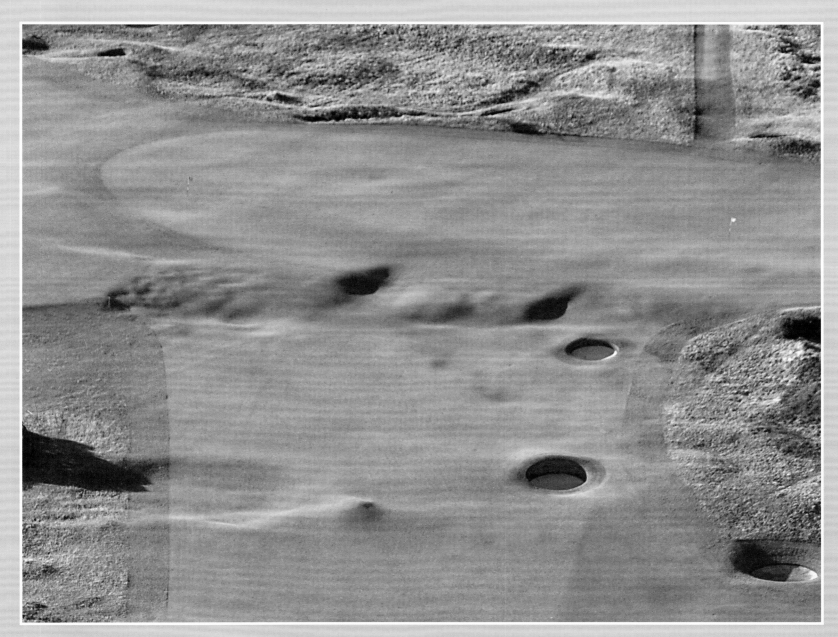

High is an apt name for the 11th, and not just because it's situated on the most elevated point of the course, for this, in the view of many, is the architectural highlight of the course. Few holes, if any, present a more captivating complex of peril than this 174-yard par three.

It offers the most straightforward and visible green on the course—no inscrutable humps or ridges, just one long, precipitous slide from left to right and back to front, a total drop of more than fifty feet—all there in plain sight.

However, there is much more to look at than just the green. Twelve-foot deep Hill bunker lies in wait on the left and gaping, vertical-faced Strath bunker is under the right wing, just in front of the habitual pin position. Pulls and hooks invariably find Hill; pushes and slices are gathered by Strath. To complicate matters, the well-struck shot that trickles even an inch off the back of the green will tumble into a deep hollow beyond. Rarely on the Old Course does one need a 60-degree wedge, but here it may be called upon for three or four consecutive shots. As Bernard Darwin observed a century ago, "… trouble once begun at this hole may never come to an end till the card is torn into a thousand fragments."

A young Bobby Jones met his match here during a qualifying round for the 1921 British Amateur Championship, taking four strokes in Hill bunker before picking up his ball and walking off the course, a mistake he referred to in his autobiography as "one last superbly childish gesture."

Since this is the most exposed point on the course, wind is constant, and its force and direction play havoc with the assignment from the tee. One local has played the hole for 40 years, never using anything but a 3-iron, while others swear they've hit everything from a driver to a wedge. The sweeping breezes combine with the severe slope to make this the most treacherous green on the course. The best adventures unfold when the wind howls out of the south-west so that even a solidly struck shot, upon hitting the putting surface, will kick sharply to the right and roll down the hill to the seventh green, leaving an uphill putt that could be 200 feet or more with 30 or 40 feet of break. In such an instance, three-putting is not a danger, it's an achievement.

No green lies closer to water than this one, just a few paces from the Eden Estuary, and in earlier days it was even closer. Back then beach sand blew up onto the green with such regularity that it filled up the hole, prompting Old Tom Morris to develop a tin cylinder to capture the ball—the invention of the putting cup.

Over the last two centuries numerous golf course architects have adopted, adapted, and copied this hole, but no replica will ever equal the original.

◀ Number 11 is one of only three tees that offer a clear view to the green (the 1st and 18th are the others) and yet this is one of the most elusive greens on the course. It is invariably the most exposed to wind and has both the most punishing bunkers and the most fiercely sloped surface, a precipitous drop from back to front.

Vertical-faced Strath bunker is just in front of the habitual
pin position. As Bernard Darwin observed a century ago,
"...trouble once begun at this hole may never come to an
end until the card is torn into a thousand fragments."

Welcome to the Mata Hari of golf holes. Sweet little Heathery is not quite what she seems.

The first-time player, often reeling from a bout with number 11, steps onto this hole and breathes a sigh of relief. The elevated tee offers a broad, clear view of the not-so-distant green. Granted there are stands of gorse on both sides, but in between them is a wide, welcoming fairway that tumbles gently to the target. A glance at the scorecard confirms the hole is pushover short, just 316 yards.

Then a closer look at the card shows this hole has been accorded the number three stroke index. "What am I missing?" he asks himself.

"Six bunkers" is the answer. Four of them lurk unseen in the middle of the landing area. Another—Admiral's—is just a few steps off the tee, ready to engorge a topped shot, and a final one cuddles into the face of a knoll, front and centre of the green.

The hole wasn't intended to look this way. For most of its life—up until the mid-twentieth century—the Old Course was played in reverse—in a clockwise circle instead of counterclockwise as it is today. This fairway thus moved in the directly opposite direction (from the current 13th tee to the current 11th green). The raised front edges of the current bunkers (which obscure them from view now) were very visible from the opposite angle.

Much rumination takes place at this tee, especially when there's crosswind or headwind. Essentially three routes are available: play either left or right of the quartet of bunkers, hoping to stay inside the cordoning rough and bushes, or attempt to take them out of play with a strong and straight shot of 225 yards.

A second slyly difficult aspect of this hole is the green. Although this is a double green with number six, it plays more like a half green when the hole is placed, as it invariably is, on the shallow back plateau, barely a dozen paces deep before it falls off the back. No matter where the drive is positioned, the approach will have to be extremely well executed—either an expertly judged bump and run or a precise lofted iron—if it is to stay on that top tier.

Several years ago Jack Nicklaus called this the best hole on the course, referring to the strategy and game management it required. Today Nicklaus would be the first to admit that, for the pros at least, number 12 poses only a shadow of its former challenge. Indeed, Tiger Woods's strategy here is to lay through, take all the bunkers and gorse out of play by slugging his teeshot to a flat area between the back right of the green and the 13th tee. That leaves either a putt or simple chip for eagle.

◄ Six bunkers hidden in the rolling 6th fairway

The Old Course ⟿ № 12

The tee of number 12 brings a distant view of home along with the last good birdie chance of the round (always assuming its minefield of invisible bunkers can be avoided).

The reverse view from the 12th green reveals all.

These days the Open Championship at St Andrews is not played on the Old Course, it is played on the Old Course, the New Course, the Eden Course and the Ladies Putting Course, known affectionately as The Himalayas.

The inexorable advancements in ball and club technology, turfgrass agronomy, and human fitness have combined to strain the seams on the Old Lady's garment, so her sister courses have been brought in to help contain the world's best players. Number 13 is the first of two consecutive holes whose championship tees now lie on the Eden, this one jutting into the right hand rough of the par-four third hole. From that championship tee, the hole plays 436 yards.

The rest of the world attacks it at 388 yards, and even at that length it is a full examination. Tom Simpson, the iconoclastic early-twentieth-century golf course architect, once called number 13 the single best hole in golf, then added, "If an architect were to lay out such a hole today he would be considered certifiable."

Without question a sound mind is helpful in addressing this puzzle that can be solved in a couple of ways. The most obvious target off the tee is a rectangular area, roughly the size of a football pitch, hemmed on the right by thick rough and gorse and on the left by a procession of pot bunkers whose names suggest their capacity for mayhem: Nick's (as in Old Nick—Satan), The Coffins (three of them), Cat's Trap, and Walkinshaw. (In general the most colourfully named bunkers tend to be

on the back nine, the "left hand" side of the course that was originally used for both outward and inward holes. Those on the front were man-made, placed at the turn of the twentieth century when the course was widened.)

At the far end of the target area, at about the 270-yard mark, the ground suddenly surges up five or six feet, blocking any view of the green. A safe and solid tee shot will stop a few yards short of this ridge, leaving about 150 yards to the hole.

A more aggressive option is to take on the bunkers with a drive into the sixth fairway, on slightly higher ground. From this angle the ridge is less of an issue and the green is partially visible. This is the kind of drive where one holds one's breath for the first two or three bounces. If the ball is still bounding happily after that, the bunkers have been eluded.

No matter what the angle of attack, several factors complicate the approach. The ground leading to the hole is extremely crumpled and unpredictable—this is no place to expect a friendly bounce—and anything short and to the left risks a visit to another feared bunker: Lion's Mouth. Meanwhile, at the right edge of the green is an even more difficult one, Hole O' Cross. Finally, the green pitches from front to back and right to left—and the pin is often positioned somewhere on the right-front. Add a bit of tailwind, and this is one of the most demanding approaches on the course.

◄ A hint of Nick's bunker and The Coffins from the 13th tee.

The double green shared by the 13th and 5th holes is the largest on the course, but finding it and then two putting can be a considerable challenge. The teeshot must be surgically accurate and when the pin is positioned at the front of the green, few mortals will be able to get close to it. Except for the 17th hole, this is the toughest par four on the home stretch.

Jack Nicklaus slept here.

In the first round of the 1995 Open Championship, the greatest golfer of all time allowed his legendarily laser-like concentration to lapse while playing this hole. The result: four bunker shots, three putts, and a quintuple-bogey 10.

It's a hole that can do that. The most peril-strewn assignment on the course, big number 14 is a sneering pirate, a sniper, a saboteur in wait. Nowhere are more rounds derailed and destroyed than at this 530-yard par five.

The first thing that catches your attention when you step onto this tee is the low stone wall running along its right side. On the other side of it, golfers blithely play the second hole of the Eden Course. As companionable as these folks may seem, you don't want to join them. So you seek comfort on the left. Over there, however, a series of dark shadows betrays more danger—a quartet of deep bunkers known as the Beardies.

If at this point you feel in need of some divine intervention, align yourself with the church spire jutting from the right side of the distant St Andrews skyline. A drive directed on that path will finish on the broad expanse of fairway known as the Elysian Fields.

◄ The broad expanse of the Elysian Fields, from the 14th tee.

But there are still 11 more bunkers, over 6,500 square feet of sand, to hurdle before reaching this green, and the largest of them—the largest on the course—lies smack in the path of your next shot. It stretches across nearly the entire width of the hole and its front wall is ten feet high. The bunker where the Golden Bear took four swings is known appropriately as Hell.

So you must make a choice—whether to be careful, canny, or courageous. If careful, you'll bunt something to the far end of the fairway, just short of the area of rough where Hell lies (along with four smaller bunkers). If cunning, you'll tack fifty yards to the left of Hell, onto the fifth fairway where a flattish area leaves a clear view and the best angle to the green. If courageous—and favoured with the necessary might and conditions— you'll smash one over Hell, maybe even all the way to the green. Any shot that strays too far left risks a visit to four more bunkers, with two more beyond the green.

But this is also a green that protects itself—its right side surges up like a cresting wave, and then spills down across the surface, sweeping golf balls along with it. Of all the goal-line defences on the Old Course, this may be the most vexing, whether you choose to attack it with a wedge, an iron or a putter. Indeed, to pull off this shot, you'll need to be careful, canny and courageous—and perhaps a bit lucky as well.

The Old Course   No 14

A quartet of deep bunkers known as The Beardies
and the broad expanse of fairway—the Elysian Fields

Hell Bunker is 23 yards wide, 23 yards long and eight feet deep at its steepest. It is an architectural marvel to be admired, but only as you walk past, never from its depths. Unless you hit a long tee shot, don't try to clear Hell with your second—lay-up short of it or play down the adjacent 5th fairway.

St Andrews has always been a men's town. From the days of the medieval priests and prelates, through a university that remained all male for 480 years, through the preponderance of fishermen, tradesmen, farmers and, of course, golfers, men have ruled. Occasionally, however, a member of the fairer sex leaves her mark, and one of them was undeniably Miss Agnes Grainger.

A century or so ago, Agnes was not only one of the better golfers in town but also something of a women's activist. In 1898 she organized a golf section of the St Rule ladies' social club and became its first captain, and five years later she convinced the Royal & Ancient Golf Club to host the first Scottish Ladies Golf Championship on the Old Course.

Her accomplishments must have been a source of chest-swelling pride, because Agnes is immortalized on the fairway of hole 15 where for decades golfers have been trying to position themselves squarely between Miss Grainger's Bosoms.

Even without those two fetching hillocks, the view from this tee is a fine one, with the full St Andrews skyline near and clear. This is also perhaps the only respite in the demanding stretch run of the back nine.

That is not to say it is without demands. As always the line of gorse looms on the right, blessedly making its final appearance. On the left a poor shot—topped or duck hooked—will find the south wing of Cottage bunker, while an unlucky one will be snagged by a little

pot known as Sutherland. In 1835 the R&A decided to cover up this bunker, but the golf-maniacal chap for whom it is named raised a persistent protest until one night a group of locals took matters into their own hands and restored it, leaving a note that read simply "Sutherland."

By the middle of the twentieth century, such nocturnal shenanigans were less easy to pull off, and when the R&A decided that another bunker in this fairway, a small pot named Hull, just to the right of Cottage, was unnecessary, it disappeared for good. That was in 1949, the last known bunker to have been removed from the Old Course.

A drive that settles happily into Agnes's cleavage will leave 140 yards to the green, with a trio of all but irrelevant bunkers lying at about the halfway point. Bernard Darwin once observed that at the Old Course, "the ground is never helping us; in its kindest mood it is no more than strictly impartial." The entry to this green brings one of those more genial places. Rather than a swale, or hollow, there is only a slight dip and rise in the ground. A lone bunker set in a small hill at the far left is the only cause for concern.

The deep green is as close to bowl-shaped as there is on the Old Course, so a slight miss to the right or left tends to collect in the low-lying centre where the pin is invariably located.

◄ The view from the 15th tee.

A trio of all but irrelevant fairway bunkers and a lone bunker on the left of the green are the only cause for concern.

Let's say you're having one of those days when you and the Old Lady are just not getting on well. You've done your best to curry her favour but nothing has worked. The gorse, the bunkers, the greens have all conspired to make you wish you were somewhere else.

Well, this tee is an excellent place to quit. It's not that the last three holes aren't worth playing, just that this patch of turf happens to be the geographic centre of golf in St Andrews. If you choose to walk off the Old Course here you can be on the first tee of any of five other courses, all within less than five minutes.

To your left, just beyond the third fairway, are the New and Jubilee. To your right, just across an out-of-bounds fence, are the Eden, Strathtyrum and Balgove. And if things are truly dire, a simple hop over that same fence will put you in the middle of a magnificent practice facility, replete with a staff of highly qualified teaching professionals ready to help you repair your game.

Should you decide to continue playing number 16, please know that the practice ground is also very accessible via your teeshot, with the out-of-bounds running the entire length of the hole. As is so often the case, however, that right-hand route—if you dare take it—will offer a more propitious angle to the green. Still, the wise advice—attributed to Jack Nicklaus—is that "only fools and amateurs go right at 16."

The left-centre of the fairway would be ideal were it not for the fact that this is the home of The Principal's Nose bunker, with two deep-set "eyes" directly behind it and another sizeable pot, Deacon Sime, a bit further on—enough to encourage most mortals to aim well left, maybe even all the way to the third fairway. Those who do will face a lengthy second shot over an expanse of heather, gorse and a pair of bunkers to a raised green with the out-of-bounds staring from beyond.

The front porch of this green is roughly four feet lower than the rest of it, so the approach, whether bumped low or hoisted high, must have sufficient force to settle on the plateau. Those who are too strong, however, will find rough, a swale, and a bunker beyond.

When the Centenary Open Championship was played here in 1960, Arnold Palmer took a characteristically aggressive approach to this hole, smashing his drive 340 yards onto the green and then holing a four-footer for eagle. That was in a practice round. Once the bell rang, Arnie, with help from caddie Tip Anderson, played it safe and nearly won his third straight major title that year. Only the champion, Australian Kel Nagle, beat him.

◄ Left centre of the 16th fairway is the home of The Principal's Nose bunker, with two deep-set eyes behind it.

The Principal's Nose bunker with an out-of-bounds right — enough to encourage most mortals to aim well left, maybe even as far as the third fairway.

If you can't hit the broad side of a barn, take heart. On this tee, you stare straight at the hindquarters of a hotel and the key is to aim at it but miss it. No par four in the world begins—or ends—quite like number 17.

The general concept of the hole is simple enough, a dogleg right where the more you can bite off, the shorter second shot and better angle you'll have to the pin. It's what pops up along the way that separates this hole from all others.

On the inside of that dogleg is the Old Course Hotel. Anyone hoping to reach the green in two must play over one of its outbuildings—a dark green one-story cottage that replicates the railway sheds that were on the same site a century ago. Those who push, slice or overreach with their drives may end up on the balcony of Room 217 or in a pint of lager in the garden of the hotel's Jigger Inn.

Even those who successfully hurdle the hotel have much more to face. The left side of this 455-yard hole is lined with the thickest rough on the course. Approach shots from that angle will have to deal with Scholars bunker, Progressing bunker, Road bunker and then at the back of the green the road itself—an increasingly more vicious parade of perils.

However it is the combination of the Road bunker and the road, pinching the smallest green on the course, that makes this one of the most daunting shots in golf. The bunker is small but its perimeter has been contoured carefully so that it gathers shots that at first appear safely outside its grasp. Even putts can be swallowed. Conversely, the relevant target area of the green—a slim plateau set on a diagonal to the fairway—is barely half the size of the green itself, about 3,500 square feet—any shot that spills beyond it will likely settle on either a shell path or a paved road, where getting up and down is about a one-in-five proposition.

Thus, there are two imperatives here. First, stay to the right, beyond the clutches of the bunker, and second, take one club less than the yardage requires. If your ball happens to find its way to the second tier, fine. If not, you'll have a short chip or putt and will have spared yourself some road rage.

The list of victims here is long and illustrious. However, in recent Open Championships the hole has lost some of its sting, as today's long-hitting professionals have begun subduing it with irons from the tee, and wedges to the green. Thus, for the 2010 Open the R&A built a new tee (on the adjacent practice ground), extending the length by 35 yards in hopes of returning the Road Hole to its former fierceness.

◄ The daunting view from the 17th tee

The Road Bunker is not large but the ground surrounding it has been craftily contoured so that any ball passing within 10 feet of it will be gathered into its lethal lair. The ensuing assignment will be to explode the ball with just enough force to clear the front lip and plop on the green—even a whisker more power and it will likely end up on the dreaded road beyond. Number 17 began its life as a par-five and for all but the very best players, it still plays that way.

While striding up this fairway, even the lowliest golfer can be forgiven if, for one brief shining moment, he imagines himself an Olympic athlete, a marathoner entering the great arena for his final glorious lap. The game of golf has thousands of better finishing holes than this one, but no more grand finale.

Following the rigours of number 17, this is unquestionably a respite—365 yards of sprawling fairway without a blade of rough, sprig of gorse or grain of sand—and therein lies its challenge. "You just can't do anything wrong on 18," says golf architect Pete Dye. "You've got to birdie it every time, only you can't."

That said, there is plenty that can go awry. The Swilken Burn, just a few yards off the tee, is not a factor except for a teeshot that is topped. What is a factor, however, is a white out-of-bounds fence lining the entire right side of the hole. When the wind is off the sea, even a slightly errant drive can quickly find a home in the Auld Grey Toon.

The ideal teeshot is struck squarely at the big red-and-gold clock on the front of the R&A clubhouse. With some luck it will avoid the asphalt aggravation of Grannie Clark's Wynd, which bisects this fairway and the first. (Like the road behind the 17th green, it is very much in play and despite being in the centre of the fairway, one is not permitted a free drop.)

In 1902 the name of this hole was changed from Home to Tom Morris, and that's only appropriate as it was he who constructed this, the largest single green on the course, moving it back some 50 yards from its original position, contouring it artfully, and creating the feature that dominates the hole: the Valley of Sin.

Today's strongest players can drive the green, just as Jack Nicklaus famously did in the 1970 Open Championship. His play-off victim that year, Doug Sanders, meanwhile stumbled sinfully through the valley, taking three strokes from 75 yards when two would have won him the title in regulation.

The 1990 champion, Nick Faldo, helped his cause greatly when, in round one, he holed a 100-foot bump and run for eagle. Five years later, Costantino Rocca experienced both agony and ecstasy on this hole. After chunking his second into the Valley of Sin, he holed his slope-climbing 40-foot putt for birdie to tie John Daly. Rocca lost the play-off but has called that birdie putt the most memorable stroke of his career.

Anyone who has sunk a long one here, in the shadow of the R&A clubhouse and with assorted onlookers ringing the green, knows exactly what Rocca means.

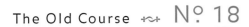

Late-evening shadows highlight the Valley of Sin at the home
green as the Royal & Ancient clubhouse basks beyond. Two
putts for par here, then perhaps a pint or two and a think back
on the day—the bunkers, blind shots, double greens and mammoth putts of a course unlike any other. Time to plan a return.

12 MUST-PLAY COURSES

THE PILGRIM'S TRAIL

CASTLE STUART

The links of Scotland are the oldest courses in the world. Indeed, the average age of the 11 courses that follow is well over a century.

And a child shall lead them.

Born in 2009, Castle Stuart has been hailed as the most significant addition to the links landscape since Turnberry debuted nearly 60 years ago. Only one other course gets the same sort of accolades—10-year-old Kingsbarns—and that's no coincidence. These are two babies with the same father.

Mark Parsinen made a fortune in the computer software industry but didn't discover his true passion until he partnered with golf course architect Kyle Phillips to build the Granite Bay golf course near his home in northern California, a design that instantly drew strong praise and high ratings.

Next Parsinen moved 7,000 miles east to the Kingdom of Fife where he once again teamed with Phillips to convert a stretch of drab farmland into the modern masterpiece that is Kingsbarns. Barely had Kingsbarns grown in when Parsinen became restless and began to comb the Caledonian coastline for a similar opportunity. To the good fortune of golfers everywhere, he found it in the Highlands, on the south shore of the Moray Firth, five minutes from Inverness Airport.

Co-designing this time with Gil Hanse, Parsinen spent five years creating Castle Stuart, applying the lessons he'd learned at Kingsbarns while exhibiting an attention to detail that extended to everything from the fringing of bunkers to the design of the windows in the men's toilet.

Central to both designers' philosophy was the conviction that a golf course should be fun—riveting, encouraging, taunting, confounding, challenging fun. At Castle Stuart the fun begins with the unique natural assets of the playground, and it's a playground not unlike a football arena—tall and tiered, with a drop of nearly 150 feet from its back row to the field. Each nine begins in the box seats at ground level (or in this case, water level) then loops inland and upland—into the mezzanine—before climbing to a finish in the upper deck.

Parsinen believes in keeping a golfer's attention, giving him something to focus on not simply during the playing of shots but in all the moments in between. Walk these holes and you walk toward the majestic Kessock Bridge and the Black Isle peninsula, toward historic Fort George and the Chanonry Lighthouse, and after playing your teeshot at the par-three fourth you walk straight toward 400-year-old Castle Stuart itself.

Broad, sparsely bunkered fairways keep everyone in the game. A poor drive will leave a difficult shot but a shot nonetheless, while a missed approach often leaves not simply a shot but a plethora of alternative shots as the cleverly sculpted greensites pose questions with multiple possible answers.

Castle Stuart   N°. 3

The third hole, a drivable par four. The more vexing peril may be greenside left where a nest of moguls, dips and sod barricades have been carefully configured so that even those who drive pin high may struggle to save par.

The par three 11th. Two large bunkers conspire
with fiendish front-right contours to make this
an extremely intimidating 130 yard shot

Six of the holes play along the firth while others seem almost to launch over it, their infinity-edged greens bleeding into the distant horizon. During construction Parsinen took pains to position his greens so that when players stand in the centre of the fairway assessing their shots, what they see is a flag flapping vividly against the backdrop of the water—not against the sky or mountains beyond but precisely against the water.

Another goal was the creation of a "landscape mosaic." Much of the Castle Stuart site was featureless farmland. To add some colour, truckloads of heather were brought in from the highland moors and local varieties of fescue were introduced on the hillocks beside the fairways.

Texture was also added through "chunking," a practice first used at Philadelphia's Merion Golf Club whereby clumps of rough native grasses were dropped randomly into the bunkers to give them a weathered look of instant maturity.

Most of the soil was rich in sand, with little major earthmoving required. The architects, however, paid close attention to the sculpting of contours—and not just for aesthetics or even linksland similitude. At the third hole, a drivable par four with a green perched on the edge of the firth, two bunkers on the right present an obvious caution. The more vexing peril, though, may be greenside left where a nest of moguls, dips, and sod barricades have been carefully configured so that even those who drive pin high may struggle to save par.

Castle Stuart measures 6,553 yards from the foremost men's tees, just over 7,000 from the tips, but there is room to take it back another 400 for a professional event.

At the first and 10th holes, the choice of tees involves both distance and elevation, as each hole can be played from a forward tee at ground level, a second one halfway up a gorse-covered cliff, or a back tee just steps from the clubhouse at the very top of the property.

With breathtaking views everywhere, it's hard to pick a signature hole but a leading candidate is surely number 11, a picturesque par three that plays straight at the water. Two large bunkers conspire with fiendish front-right contouring to make this an extremely intimidating 130-yard shot, especially when the wind is off the firth.

The most manufactured hole is the 12th, a firth-side par five that plays steeply uphill. It was created totally by bulldozers as a way of getting golfers back to the higher reaches of the course. The climb continues with an extremely taxing walk from this green to the next tee—but once again, Parsinen has thought of everything; halfway up the hill is a soda machine and everyone gets a free drink.

The 16th hole is a gentle dogleg left of 335 yards. Downwind it's easily drivable—a par 3.5. However, that will mean the next hole, doubling back 224 yards into the breeze, is also a par 3.5. At the clifftop 18th, also into the wind and 595 yards, even the strongest player will need three good shots to get home in two.

Castle Stuart may be just a baby but already she stands shoulder to shoulder with the very best links in the world.

Castle Stuart ⊷ № 13

The bunker-free approach to number
13 set against the Keswick Bridge

Castle Stuart ⤬ № 18

The distant green may lull the unwary
to try for the green in two but it will
take a shot of both power and precision.
Anything that falls short will mean a
struggle if par five is to be achieved.

CARNOUSTIE

Within the English language, a rare few words have the capacity to strike fear in a golfer's heart. One of them is "shank." Another is "Carnoustie." Twelve miles across the North Sea from St Andrews, in a dour little town that can seem older and greyer than the Old Grey Town itself, lies the sternest assignment in Open Championship golf.

Carnoustie is the full examination. At the same time, it is a fair and true measurement. Its fairways are humpy but not bumpy, its greens contoured but not sloped. Crazy bounces are few as are blind shots, and at no time do more than two consecutive holes play in the same direction, so this is a challenge that is balanced, no matter how the wind may blow.

Wind, however, is a major factor here, narrowing a long course (7,361 yards from the back tees) whose holes are lined by every manner of peril—out-of-bounds, trees, heather, gorse, fescue, dry ditches and a pair of burns that come into play on a third of the holes and into mind on half of them.

The nature of the assignment becomes clear immediately via a par four of 401 yards into the prevailing wind, with out-of-bounds left, bunkers right, and a burn just in front of the tee—and this is one of the easier holes. There will be no relaxing until the 19th.

Carnoustie's first five holes are par fours, each changing direction and no two of them remotely alike. Number two is a beautiful rightward dogleg through shouldering sandhills, the tee shot complicated by a single bunker staring back from the centre of the fairway. The shortest two-shotter comes at 337-yard number three, named Jockie's Burn for the little stream that crosses in front of a heavily contoured green that falls off to bunkers on both sides. If ever a crisply struck approach shot is needed, it is here.

It's back into the wind at the fourth, bending gently past well-positioned bunkers to a long narrow green shared with the 14th hole, the only double green on the course. Then at number five, heather and bunkers narrow the fairway while Jockie's Burn returns to shorten it, cutting across at the 300-yard mark.

Carnoustie is a course for strong, straight driving, nowhere more so than at the par-five sixth where the view from the tee includes a pair of bunkers in the middle of the fairway, an out-of-bounds fence to the left, and a burn to the right, all of it playing into the prevailing wind. The demands increase as the hole progresses, with the burn piercing into the fairway a few yards short of the angled and heavily-bunkered green. This is the hole made famous as Hogan's Alley because of the four straight birdies Ben Hogan made here en route to victory in the 1953 Open.

The inward nine begins with an American style hole, its green guarded by trees and encircled by water. "South America" allegedly got its name because of a local lad

◄ At the short par four 3rd hole, Jockie's Burn is the key feature

Carnoustie ⤢ Nº 6

Hole number 6, Hogan's Alley. The view from the tee
is daunting: out-of-bounds left, bunkers centre, and a
burn to the right, all of it played invariably into the wind.
For most mortals, a par five here is a very welcome score.

CARNOUSTIE

The par five 14th, stroke index one. Bunkering and
out-of-bounds on the dogleg left, with the impressive
Spectacle bunkers to be cleared in two or three.

named David Nicoll who announced he was emigrating to that far-off land, then over-celebrated at his bon voyage party the night before his trip and, instead of making his train, fell asleep in a copse of trees beside the 10th hole. When it plays into the wind, this is one of the hardest par fours in Great Britain.

If there's a let-up on the back nine it is the 14th, a short par five dominated at its halfway point by a pair of deep bunkers set in the face of a sandhill. These are the "Spectacles" for which the hole is named and, ironically, the shot over them is blind. The only major difficulty is gauging the distance to the flag on this long green that spills from its front into the green of the fourth.

Several men have had a hand in the design of Carnoustie, beginning with Allan Robertson who plotted a ten-hole course in 1850. A quarter-century later Old Tom Morris extended it to 18 and in 1926 James Braid put his stamp on it. The finishing, touch, however, came from a local architect, James Wright, who re-jigged the last few holes to create what is arguably the most fearsome finish in golf.

It begins with the 15th, a slightly right-to-left dogleg of 472 yards that calls for a draw off the tee and a fade into the half-hidden green. If you're playing a match, this would be a good place to win it, because the next three holes tend to beat everyone.

Sixteen, at 248 yards, is the longest par three in the Open rotation. With the Barry Burn and two bunkers to the left and three more bunkers to the right, this sloping sliver of a green requires a shot that is both far and sure. In 1975, when Tom Watson won the first of his five Open titles in a playoff over Jack Newton, he failed to make par on this hole in five attempts.

"Island" is the name of number 17 and it refers not to the green but the fairway, which is criss-crossed twice by the Barry Burn, leaving a sanctuary of 50 yards or so in which to position the drive. Then it's another 200 yards to the green guarded on the right front by a trio of bunkers. This hole changes markedly with a wind, as evidenced by Tiger Woods's play in the 1995 Scottish Open. On successive days, he played it with back-to-back 5-irons and back-to-back drivers.

Carnoustie's 18th will be forever linked in infamy with Frenchman Jean van de Velde, who arrived at the 72nd tee of the 1999 Open Championship with a three-stroke lead, only to take an inglorious triple-bogey seven and then lose in a playoff to Paul Lawrie. It's a lengthy and peril-packed hole, but when downwind it's reachable with a middle iron, assuming the out-of-bounds left and the insidious Barry Burn right can once more—actually twice more—be avoided; a sizable assumption, to be sure. A finishing par— like any par at Carnoustie—will be extremely well earned.

Carnoustie ∽ № 16

Number 16, at 248 yards, is the longest
par three on the Open rotation.

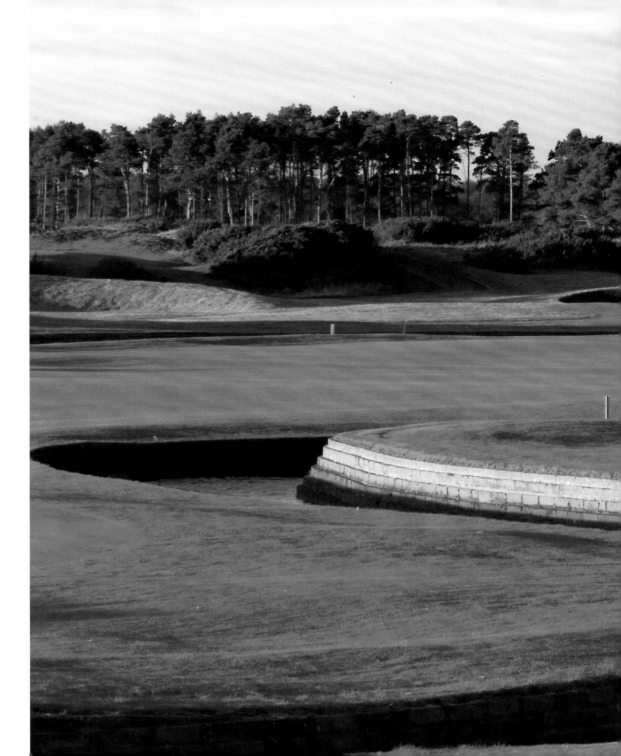

Carnoustie ⤳ № 17

The 17th is criss-crossed twice by the
Barry Burn, leaving a sanctuary of 50 yards
or so in which to position your drive.

CRUDEN BAY

Mention Cruden Bay and even the most serious golfer, if he has played it, will smile—maybe even giggle. No course charms its visitors quite like this one.

Situated on a narrow strip of sandhills between the North Sea and the town that shares its name, Cruden Bay was commissioned by the Great Scottish Northern Railway, when rail travel expanded at the end of the nineteenth century. A lavish Turnberry-style hotel came with it and before long this remote little village, 23 miles above Aberdeen, had become a popular seaside playground.

Old Tom Morris did the original design, but the man who gave this course its true character was a true character himself: Tom Simpson. A Cambridge-educated lawyer and scratch golfer, Simpson came from a privileged background and was something of a London dandy—he wore an embroidered cape, a beret, horn-rimmed sunglasses and travelled to his job sites in a silver Rolls Royce. Among his clients were the Duke of Windsor, Lord Mountbatten and two Barons de Rothschild. Fittingly perhaps, he is best remembered for his work at Morfontaine, the most exclusive golf club in France.

Bold, unorthodox, flamboyant, outlandish—those are words that describe Tom Simpson and they apply equally well to Cruden Bay. This is a course that grabs you by the lapels the moment you see it and never lets go, where virtually every hole has an element of quirkiness, a foible or surprise to be endured and enjoyed. There are hillocks to be hurdled, burns to be hopped,

mountains to be climbed, bells to be rung, puzzles to be solved. Blind shots, buffeting breezes, bad bounces—all the trademarks of links golf—are magnified here. Indeed at times the game can seem more like pinball than golf, but what a joyous game it is. Even the hole names— Whaupshank, Finnyfal, Blin' Wallie—are pure fun.

But make no mistake, there is also great and noble golf to be found here, beginning with the stretch of holes four through six—a riverside par three to a green cradled by sandhills and backdropped by the sea; a 455-yard par four that ploughs over and through a herd of camel-hump dunes; and a par five called Bluidy Burn, its green tucked around a bend, with an invisible stream crossing a few yards in front of it.

It is in the home stretch that the fun truly begins. Fourteen, a blind and terrifyingly narrow par four, plays between sandhills and the sea to a green site that could be an arena for extreme skateboarding. Fifteen is the rarest of all assignments, a blind near-dogleg par three that plays around a hillside, while in the centre of the drive zone at 17 is what appears to be a grass-covered Moby Dick. Avoid him from the tee or the second shot will have to be played over his arching back.

Eccentric as it all is, this is the stuff of intoxicating golf. In the words of Bernard Darwin, Cruden Bay is "… a place extraordinarily difficult to keep away from for those who have once come under its spell."

◄ Cruden Bay 16th green, bottom left, with the 7th green above it and the 17th, playing up the left, towards the 18th & clubhouse

The 15th green, on the right, viewed from the 16th tee. Both holes are relatively uncomplicated; the 17th (below), however, offers a completely different challenge. Few holes call for a tee shot that avoids the middle of the fairway, but that is what must be done here if the mammoth mound is to be avoided.

For those misguided souls who, for whatever imponderable reasons, are happy to walk great distances without striking a ball, Scotland's East Neuk offers a rare opportunity—a 63-mile coastal path that winds from St Andrews scenically southward all the way to the Forth Road Bridge. Happily, that route is equally attractive to golfers, as it is dotted with a dozen fine courses. Among them, one clearly stands out—Kingsbarns.

This is the Eliza Doolittle of golf courses. A decade ago it was an abandoned potato farm; now it ranks among the top 100 courses in the world. Its Professor Higgins was Mark Parsinen, a laser-focused California businessman who partnered with architect Kyle Phillips and spent the better part of four years manufacturing a links—the most man-made links ever.

Man-made, but far from fake. With authenticity as their goal, Parsinen and Phillips did their homework, visiting the best links of Great Britain and Ireland, taking notes and photos, and funnelling it all into their routing and shaping of the 18 holes.

The terrain they had may not have been distinguished but the site was spectacular, a lofty hillside spilling to the coastline. What they did was bulldoze that hill—essentially scraped the middle out of it—leaving a high shelf of holes with stunning views and a lower section, hard by the sea. Millions of cubic yards of earth were moved and sculpted, but when it was all finished Kingsbarns looked as if it had been in place for centuries, its fairways and greens fashioned by nothing more than the wind.

The first tee is at the very top of the property, but after that par four you're quickly on the lower tier. Only a ridge of low sandhills separates golfers from the sea at the par-three second, a mid-iron shot to a green that slopes from back to front and left to right toward a trio of grasping bunkers. The next hole, a par five, continues through a dune-flanked valley to a raised green that is reachable in two. But even more reachable is a cavernous bunker to the front-right, and the terrain slopes so fiercely in that direction that even putts occasionally stray into the sandy abyss.

Then it's back to the top tier for a par four that offers a choice—gamble with a 220-yard carry over a grand canyon of sand, or play safely to the right and leave yourself a longer approach. The target is an infinity-edge green, silhouetted against the North Sea. If you peer at it long enough you'll swear that Pythagoras was wrong and the earth is flat.

One of golf's most fun holes comes at the sixth where, with a following wind, a solid draw, and a bit of luck, even a medium-length hitter can land his drive on the distant hillside and see it bound merrily onto the

An aerial view of the par five 3rd hugging the coastline, with the 4th on the upper level. There is, of course, a coastal path for those misguided souls....

open-front amphitheatre green. No one, however, will drive the uphill seventh. In fact it will take a pair of solid strikes to get home on this 470-yard par four.

Pacing is a key factor at Kingsbarns—easy holes are usually followed by hard ones; short holes by long ones. After tiny number eight, just a flip wedge or 9-iron, comes the par-five ninth, climbing 558 yards back to the clubhouse. In 2003, England's Lee Westwood made history here during the Dunhill Links Championship (which Kingsbarns co-hosts with Carnoustie and the Old Course). Needing a birdie to set a course record of 64, he holed his 4-iron second shot for an albatross and 62.

There's a lengthy but not unpleasant walk from the 11th green—down and through a little forest, over a burbling stream and then back steeply uphill—to the tee of number 12, but what you behold on arrival is worth the trek. A par five that is as spectacularly beautiful as it is fun to play, it arcs gently leftward 606 yards along the craggy shoreline, culminating in an enormous angled green where the difference between a front and back pin can be three or even four clubs.

Once again short follows long with a downhill par three at 13. Then after a breather par four at number 14, it's back to the water for the toughest assignment on the course. From the back tee number 15 plays 212 yards and it is one hundred percent carry, for there is no fairway on this hole, just rocks, beach, and sea, one of the most enthralling tableaus in links golf.

Things ease up again (but only slightly) at the par five 16th, where the worst peril is unseen: an insidious little burn that grips the right and rear of the green. Then it's two stern par fours to finish. Number 17 curves to the right and then heads steeply uphill to a plateau green that does not suffer foolish shots. The 444-yard 18th is borderline criminal, with its green perched at the far edge of a bank that plummets straight into a hidden burn from which there is no recovery. Into a wind, even laying up on his hole is difficult.

Indeed, testing holes abound on Kingbarns, but the fairways are wide, the rough is generally sparse, and virtually every lie is playable—no matter how badly a shot has been played there is usually room for redemption, for hope.

And there is always a view of the sea. Modern environmental restrictions being what they are, it's highly unlikely that any more of the Fife coastline will become available for links golf. Sad as that is, there is consolation in knowing that the best was saved for last.

At the par five 12th length is important, but those who are too greedy will bring the beach into play.

Kingsbarns ⚘ № 15

One of the most daunting par three teeshots, especially when the flag is out on the point to the right and a full 180-yard carry is required. There is the optional safe play down the tree-lined left side, leaving a difficult up and down. Either way this is a full challenge.

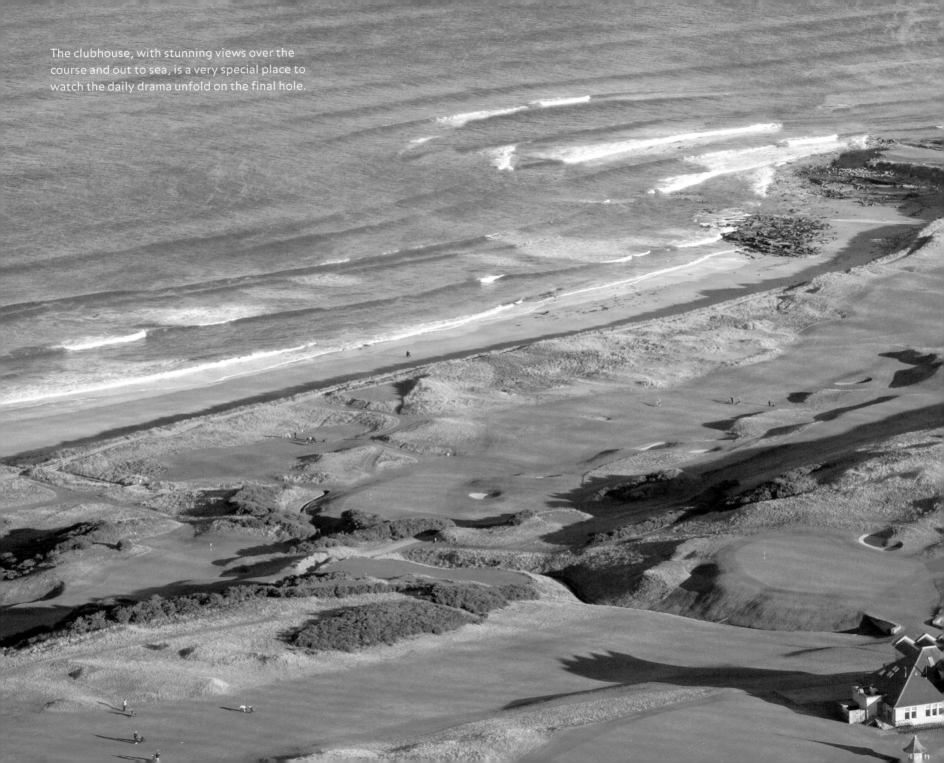

The clubhouse, with stunning views over the course and out to sea, is a very special place to watch the daily drama unfold on the final hole.

MUIRFIELD

In 1979, when *GOLF* magazine released its first-ever ranking of the top golf courses in the world, the course that led the list—ahead of Pine Valley, Pebble Beach, Royal Melbourne and all the rest—was Muirfield. To many, it was a shock that a major U.S. magazine would bestow its highest honour on a Scottish links. Yet at the same time it made sense, for this fine and fair golf course is as close to American as a links can get.

Strictly speaking, Muirfield stretches the definition of a links. It is not seaside; it sits well above and removed from the Firth of Forth, which comes into view only occasionally. Ancient stone walls and trees form its boundary on three sides, creating an enclosed, parkland feel. The fairways are relatively flat and unrumpled, all but bereft of the uneven lies and capricious bounces of traditional links. There are no burns to cross, no thickets of gorse and buckthorn to battle, no towering dunes to scale. This may not be "an auld water meadie" as the acid-tongued St Andrews defender Andra Kirkcaldy once characterized it, but it is as its name says: a moor field.

In contrast to the traditional out-and-back routing of a links course, the front nine returns to the clubhouse. In fact even the venerable club itself—the Honourable Company of Edinburgh Golfers—with its restrictive guest policy (Tuesdays and Thursdays only) and emphasis on fine food and wine, is more akin to the leading clubs of the U.S. than those of Great Britain. It's no wonder that so many Americans love Muirfield.

The first tee bears witness to another anomaly for a links course: a call for accurate driving. The most difficult opening hole on the Open Championship rota, this 446-yard par four turns gently right with a large horseshoe-shaped bunker waiting at its outside corner. The entire right side of the hole is lined with thick rough which, depending on the season and conditions, can be ankle to knee height. With bunkers front left and right, the green welcomes only a well-played shot, so the message is clear: find the fairway or pay a price.

Accuracy is equally important at the par threes. The narrow tabletop target at the 182-yard fourth falls off steeply on all sides with ferocious bunkers front and left. Distance precision is also required, as this green is 40 yards in depth. Depending on wind and pin position, it can call for anything from a short iron to a full driver.

Most of the tees at Muirfield are at least slightly elevated, offering an open view of everything to be tackled. A set of wooden steps leads from the fourth green to the tee of the first of three superb par fives, a slope-climbing 510 yards where the clear and present danger is sand (no fewer than 15 bunkers line this hole).

The bunkers at Muirfield are equally renowned for their beauty and their severity. Most of the fairway

◄ The narrow tabletop target at the 182 yard fourth falls off steeply on all sides with ferocious bunkers front and left.

The front nine finishes with a stern
par five — often played into wind

bunkers have cambered front edges at fairway height—often
there is no sand or siding visible, just a shadowy face, an
intimidating hint of doom. Often a bunker or pair of bunkers
will appear 50–100 yards short of the green, complicating the
second shot, no matter the wind direction. Those at greenside
tend to be deep—deep enough that players standing in them
cannot see the putting surface—and their steep, revetted faces
are difficult to scale, even in the age of the 60-degree wedge.

If the cluster of bunkers to the right side of the landing area
on number five can be avoided, this becomes a birdie opportunity, and for some even better. In the 1972 Open Championship,
Johnny Miller took everything out of play—even the green—
when he holed his second shot for an albatross.

When Old Tom Morris first laid out Muirfield in 1891, he
broke with links tradition. Instead of routing nine holes out and
nine back he created a pair of concentric loops, the outer front
nine circling clockwise, the inner back nine moving counter-
clockwise. By the time the teeshot is played to the par-3 7th,
the first loop is essentially complete and every kind of helping,
hurting or quartering wind has been experienced.

With no water hazards, chasms, or nettled brush to leap,
Muirfield is not a course that offers many risk-reward moments.
Solid, careful shotmaking is what works—it's no surprise that
methodical Nick Faldo won two of his Open titles here, the
second of them after a final round of 18 straight pars. For years
there was an opportunity to gamble at the eighth hole, a dogleg
par four where long hitters could cut the corner with a bold
drive, but after Walter Hagen did this a bit too successfully
en route to victory in the 1929 Open, trees and bushes were
planted in the right-hand rough.

The front nine finishes with a stern par five—often played
into the wind—with an out-of-bounds wall left, the omnipres-
ent thick fescue rough to the right, and a gauntlet of ingeniously

placed bunkers commanding attention along the line of play. A five here is always well earned.

Remarkably, the only blind drive on the course comes at the 11th where a high ridge conceals the landing area. Once that ridge has been climbed, however, the reward is a panoramic view of the Firth of Forth. The tiered green is ringed with a garland of bunkers.

Muirfield greens are not wildly contoured but they are full of broad and subtle slopes and their speed and smoothness is unsurpassed in the British Isles. Together with the crisp-edged bunkers they present a neatly-tailored, cleaned-and-pressed look that is consistent with this club.

The most photographed holes are the two inward par threes, each playing slightly uphill to a green surrounded by bunkers. During the 2002 Open Championship, Ernie Els had final-round adventures at both of them, playing a brave explosion to two feet to save par at 13, then double-bogeying 16 to lose his lead before winning a four-way playoff.

But no hole has produced more championship drama than the 17th, a reachable dogleg par five with deep bunkers to be avoided on both the drive and second shot. The putting surface sits in a bowl formed by shouldering hills. It was here in 1972 that Lee Trevino, thinking he was out of contention, played an almost list-less chip from the back of the green that somehow found the cup. A stunned Tony Jacklin then three-putted from short range and Trevino stole the title.

Number 18—like all of Muirfield—is a stern and straight-forward assignment: 465 yards of fescue-lined fairway heading straight at another staunchly bunkered and slippery green, with the iconic clubhouse just behind.

From beginning to end, there is no nonsense at Muirfield— just a full and unrelenting examination of one's game.

Muirfield's two nines run in a pair of concentric circles, the front nine heading clockwise and the back nine, within it, counter-clockwise. They do, however, meet up at one point, and the greens of the 5th and 11th holes could be combined as one were they not both ringed by bunkers.

Muirfield ↜ № 18

Muirfield, at first blush, may seem an unremarkable links, without the seaside splendour of Turnberry, the raw challenge of Carnoustie, or the quirky charm of St Andrews, but there is no fairer or more complete examination of one's game than here. Well-planned, crisply played shots will be rewarded, deviations will be punished. Muirfield finds you out in a way that few courses do.

North Berwick

The Old Course, Prestwick and North Berwick have been called living museums of golf. If that's true, surely the most captivating exhibits are at North Berwick. You see a few things here that you simply can't find anywhere else.

The collection of rarities begins at the very first hole. Where else does the opening assignment entail back-to-back blind shots, a long-iron lay up into a hollow, followed by wedge up the face of a cliff? Before you can catch your breath the second hole brings a tee shot across rocks, sand and sea. A battered wooden fence separates all this from the fairway, but should your ball stray onto the beach, you're welcome to hop over and give it a whack.

Next comes a 460-yard par four where the advice is "aim your tee shot at the gap in the wall." You won't reach that ancient stone barrier, but your next shot will have to hurdle it. Number four is a par three to a sunken green—nothing odd or unusual here except the strong possibility of being bombarded by a teeshot from the adjacent 14th hole.

Yes, North Berwick is a collection of architectural artifacts. To walk this land is to walk back two centuries in time, to an era when the golf course designer—in this case David Strath—did the best he could with what Mother Nature provided him. But if it is at times

bewildering it is also beguiling. Few museums living or otherwise can boast a more splendid setting.

Nineteen miles due south of St Andrews and 15 miles from Edinburgh, North Berwick occupies an ideal perch on the south shore of the Firth of Forth just at the point where it melts into the North Sea. The view from these fairways includes not only the water of the firth but the hills of Fife and the Isle of May. Just to the east, rising 350 feet out of the sea is the volcanic hill known as Bass Rock, while looming on the inland flank is 650-foot Berwick Law. With all this natural beauty competing for attention, keeping one's head down becomes a true act of will.

The course takes its path in a sort of lopsided figure eight with the first and last three holes forming the smaller loop and holes four through 15 the larger. An out-of-bounds wall haunts the left side of holes four through nine, but the quirks and oddities ebb through this stretch, except at the seventh green where the menagerie of peril includes a burn in front, deep grass to the rear, bunkers to the right and another stone wall to the left.

With back-to-back par fives at eight and nine, the course reaches its western extremity and also returns to the edge of the shore. The par three 10th plays from a tee high in the sandhills and sets the stage for a dramatic—and once again quirky—finishing stretch.

◄ The 2nd fairway and green.

Number 13 appears to be a perfectly straightforward hole—a quietly bending par four of 388 yards—until you see what needs to be dealt with on the approach shot; yet another wall, this one stretched demonically across the very front of the green. Squeezing the green from the rear is a tall sandhill and behind that is the sea. To over-hit this green is surely not a good thing, but the course guide says it all: "Don't argue with the wall, it's older than you."

"Perfection" is the name of the 14th hole, but surely that refers more to its ideal setting than its architectural flawlessness. Like the first hole it calls for two blind shots, the first to a narrow, wickedly humpy fairway and the second—a pure act of faith—over a hump to a runaway green that sits on the very edge of the sea. "Hit and Hope" would have been a more suitable name.

Like all good museums, North Berwick has a main attraction, a work of art revered above all the others, a treasure that has been copied over and over. That is hole 15, the Redan. The term "redan" is borrowed from the French and refers to a kind of parapet or fortress. The salient characteristic of North Berwick's Redan is its wide, shallow green, set on a diagonal to the line of play, the higher right-front portion closer to the tee than the lower left-rear. Three deep bunkers on the right and one at front left, add to the complexity of the shot.

A strategically brilliant design that works its wiles particularly well in windy conditions, the 15th may call for anything from a high, green-gripping fade to a low running draw, depending upon wind condition and pin placement. Architect C.B. Macdonald copied this hole at National Golf Links and Chicago Golf Club and numerous other replicas dot courses around the U.S.

If the 15th hole is famous, the 16th is notorious. Yet another wall surfaces on the teeshot of this 380-yard par four and there is a burn to contend with as well, running across the fairway at about the 230-yard mark. But the hole's most malevolent quirk is its green, which is actually more like three greens in one. Imagine two upturned coffee cups separated by an angled butter dish, and you'll have some idea of what awaits. To hit and hold this surface is a major achievement—to two-putt it, especially from one cup to the other, is something between a miracle and an accident.

Number 17 is a strong, conventional par four, the second half of it climbing up to a plateau near the first green. This would have been a better finishing hole than what is there now, a driveable little par four across a broad, flat fairway. Still, with the green backdropped by the clubhouse, the gabled roofs of the town, and the magnificence of Berwick Law, it's a very pleasant last 300 yards. And there is one remaining danger—in the mode of the Old Course—a white out-of-bounds fence down the right side, separating the golf course from the town. One false move on this teeshot, and you could put a dent in your very own vehicle.

North Berwick ✦ № 14

The blind approach 14th green "Perfection" perched on the water's edge, the intimidating 15th Redan to the right.

The 16th begins with a teeshot over a burn but the real terror is its fiendish three-tiered green. The finishing hole (right), in the manner of the Old Course, is a short par four with out-of-bounds right and an entire town looming beyond.

Prestwick, despite being one of the world's most elite private clubs, is a welcoming sort of place. A splendid changing room is available just for visitors, and one and all are invited to partake of the club's excellent food and drink.

First-time players are well advised to book an early afternoon round preceded by lunch, in order that they may take full advantage of that food and drink— especially the drink. Indeed, two or three large glasses of claret might be in order. Why? Because the opening assignment at this course is one of the most terrifying shots imaginable. A free, fearless swing will be a vital asset, no matter by what means it must be induced.

It is not a long hole—just 346 yards. No, the trepidation here comes not from length but width. When you stand on this tee you look straight down both a fairway and a railway, the two of them separated by nothing but a few yards and a stone wall. The slightest push, fade or breath of sea breeze and your opening teeshot could smash through the window of the 2:12 to Glasgow. There is no bail-out to the left, just duneland dense with gorse, heather, and sand, along with a daunting view of the green, its right edge backed against the wall. This is one links hole where nothing but a string straight teeshot will do.

◄ Prestwick's opening hole

Prestwick's opener dates to the 1870s and that makes it one of the newer holes at a club that was founded in 1851. St Andrews may be the birthplace of golf but this is the birthplace of championship golf, the Open Championship having been played here for the first time in 1860. Prestwick went on to hold the first dozen Opens, with Old and Young Tom Morris winning six of them.

Back then this was a 12-hole course but the first hole was just as daunting—a "bogey 6" of 578 yards. In winning his third title Young Tom somehow managed to make a three on that hole—and that was in the days of hickory clubs and guttie balls.

Prestwick held the last of its 24 Opens in 1925. Today the course lacks the length and the club lacks the infrastructure necessary to host a modern professional championship. However, this par 71 of 6,910 yards remains a comprehensive if somewhat quirky challenge as well as a monument to the beginnings of links golf.

Seven of the original greens remain in play today, including the tiny target at number three, a par five that plays famously across The Cardinal, an immense cross bunker whose high front wall is buttressed by wooden sleepers. There is an old story of a match in which one player came to grief in that bunker, bouncing shot after shot off the planks.

"How many have you played?" his opponent called down to him from the fairway above.

"I don't know," he said. "I came in here at half past eleven and I've been hitting ever since. It's now ten minutes to 12—you work it out."

Eighteen unique golf holes, shoe-horned into one medium-sized piece of rugged linksland. This aerial view shows 14 greens. The layout is unusual, and not just because of the railway line tight on the first. Its routing moves away from the clubhouse, skirts the burn and then around the perimeter of the property coming back to the clubhouse at number 14. A brief two-hole foray leads out to the middle ground before turning homeward once more and possibly the easiest finishing hole in golf.

The fourth hole, created by Old Tom Morris when he enlarged the course to 18 holes, is said to be golf's first dogleg, and a gem it is, arcing rightward with the Pow Burn in play along the length of the inside edge. There are five doglegs on the course; curiously they all move from left to right.

Blind shots are the norm at Prestwick, but none is more sightless than the 206-yard teeshot at number five, up over an immense sandhill and down to a tightly bunkered green with nothing but a marker as a guide.

The next four par fours play on higher ground beside the railway and Glasgow Prestwick Airport. Their fairways are generally flat, in contrast to the unrelenting humpiness of the opening stretch; as such the golf is both more honest and less interesting.

Number 10 returns back over the Himalayas and Pow Burn, a stiff four of 454 yards into the prevailing breeze. The best part of the par-three 11th is the view, which includes the sea to the right and the gables and spires of Prestwick town in the distance.

Number 14 returns to the clubhouse and then begins The Loop, a circuit of four pars that average just 327 yards but have an uncanny capacity to unravel a round. The 15th presents a side-sloping fairway that plays even narrower than it looks. Number 16, only 288 yards, can be driven easily but a miss to the right may find Cardinal's bunker from nearby number three. Lurking on the left is the bunker known as Willie Campbell's Grave, where Campbell, leading the 1887 Open Championship, took four shots to escape and thereby lost to Willie Park Jr.

Then it's up and over the Alps, probably the most famous blind par four in golf. If your teeshot finds the narrow gorse-lined fairway you'll be looking straight at a 30-foot-high sandhill, which might be just as well because what lies on the other side of it is rather fearsome, a wildly sloped green fronted by a mammoth sleeper-faced bunker called Sahara. This hole is virtually unchanged since the first Open was played here 150 years ago.

In the manner of several links courses—St Andrews, North Berwick, Crail, and Brora come to mind—Prestwick all but runs out of room after 17 holes. The closing par four is thus shoehorned into 284 yards. It's very drivable, but so is the old stone clubhouse beyond, at a penalty of stroke and distance.

Late evening sun shadows the course, the 3rd flag to the left, the 12th, 16th and 18th flags and clubhouse to the right.

Prestwick ↜ № 16

Number 16 is only 288 yards long but lurking to the left is Willie Campbell's Grave bunker and to the right Cardinal's bunker.

Prestwick ᣭ № 17

Sahara bunker guards the blind
approach to the 17th green.
Beyond is the short par four 18th.

Back in the summer of 1908, a young man named Harry Lumsden took it upon himself to play nine rounds of golf—162 holes—in a single day. Incredibly, he not only completed his task, he did so with an average 18-hole score of 82. Perhaps most impressive of all, the course on which he achieved this feat was Royal Aberdeen.

Granted, a century ago Royal Aberdeen wasn't quite the test it is today, a course described by Bernard Darwin as "much more than good golf, a noble links." But remember, Harry was playing his golf with hickories and gutties—it could not have been an easy 30 or so miles he covered. Still, on a fine clear day Royal Aberdeen is hard to match, no matter how many holes you may choose to play.

Stretched beneath a line of tall coastal dunes just north of Aberdeen, this is a links in the classic mould: two parallel strings of holes, nine out and nine back. The first nine is nothing short of superb, beginning with a glorious par four that starts from a hilltop tee, just five paces from the white slate-roofed clubhouse and tumbles down a broad fairway to a green set against the North Sea and the sky.

The 1st approach

Thereafter the course turns ninety degrees left on a northward path. The next eight holes are links golf at its purest—ridge-top tees, rampantly rumpled fairways and smallish, softly contoured greens, most of them tucked into hillocks and dells. Circular, crisply revetted-

bunkers—steep in front, shallow in back—dot the path, stands of heather and gorse following alongside, and now and then a burn wanders into play. It all unfurls in a long, deep valley framed by immense sandhills.

The leftward bend of hole number two calls for a draw from the tee, but no matter where the drive may finish, the next shot is daunting—just in front of the green of this par five is an area that looks like the burial ground for a herd of pachyderms. The same sort of wild terrain separates the tee from the punchbowl green at the third, a par three that plays 248 yards from its back tee, high in the dunes. Then comes the number-one stroke hole, a 450-yard par four played through a murderously slim fairway that cascades into a gulley on its right side before arriving at a small green cinched tightly by bunkers. For the uninitiated, this stretch of the journey is rife with trap doors and pitfalls. Indeed, when playing Royal Aberdeen for the first time, it's best to be in the company of either a caddie or a seasoned member of the club.

Strong and ambitious players are welcome to take a crack at the green of the short par four fifth but the slightest miscue will bring an encounter with deep fescue or dense shrubbery. (It's appropriate that the suggestion of a five-minute time limit on searching for golf balls first came from this club.)

This aerial view shows the opening
2nd, 3rd, 4th and 5th holes.

The two sizeable bunkers that stare back from the middle of the sixth fairway, complicate the teeshot strategy—no matter which way the wind is blowing—and two more protect the right-hand entry to another narrow green. However, the most sand-intense hole is number eight, a 147-yard par three that heads briefly back south to a green ringed by no fewer than 10 bunkers.

The mighty 9th starts from a tee high in the dunes and doglegs 465 yards to the right and uphill, culminating at a two-tiered green that abuts the neighbouring Murcar Golf Club, a fine links on its own. Members of both clubs love to tell the story of the group of first-time Royal Aberdeen visitors who reached the ninth green and, instead of turning back for home, continued their journey north, eventually ending up at the wrong clubhouse.

The back nine, played on flatter, higher ground that is almost heathland in character, lacks the magic of the front. In addition, the fine sea views to the east get some unpleasant competition from industrial plants, oil rigs, and shopping malls to the west. That said, these holes lack neither interest nor challenge.

Out-of-bounds on the right side haunts number 12, where the second shot is complicated by a ridge that cuts diagonally in front of the plateau green. Thirteen starts with a blind teeshot and ends with a round-shouldered green that lives to reject approach shots. At number 14, a stream comes into play on the drive and the second must deal with a wall of earth that angles across from the left side.

Downwind on a fast-running day, the bowl green of the 15th would be drivable were it not sealed off by a deep and steep cross bunker that looks like the little brother of Hell Bunker at St Andrews.

For scenic splendour, the standout on the back nine is clearly number 17, a par three that plays straight to the sea, its three-tiered green sharing attention with the distant fishing boats and oil tankers that symbolize Aberdeen's two commercial mainstays. Then for the finish it's a muscular par four—440 yards uphill to the clubhouse, a green bunkered closely on both sides.

Play Royal Aberdeen once and, like marathon man Harry Lumsden, you'll want to play it again and again.

The par three 3rd hole, from green to tee.

Nine bunkers surround the 8th green and, depending on wind conditions, this tee shot could be anything from a 3-iron to a wedge.

Royal Aberdeen ⤳ Nº 17

Another great par three. The 17th green has bunkers front, right and left, a fall-off at the back, and even if you hit the putting surface, it is on three levels and getting it down in two is no mean feat.

For nearly a century it was links golf's best kept secret. Only during the last forty years or so has Royal Dornoch drawn the attention it deserves, and even today it remains Great Britain's least celebrated championship course.

Geography is the reason. Six hundred miles north of London, 220 miles north of Edinburgh and 60 miles north of Inverness, Dornoch is in the height of the Highlands. However, thanks to a microclimate created by the Gulf Stream, golf is played here year round, and has been for nearly four hundred years.

It was the American golf writer Herbert Warren Wind who put Royal Dornoch on the map when, in a 1964 article for The New Yorker, he rhapsodized over the course, declaring "no golfer has completed his education until he has played and studied Royal Dornoch." Gradually, serious golfers began to check it out. When Tom Watson paid a visit, made three trips around the course in 24 hours and said, "this is the most fun I've ever had playing golf," Royal Dornoch's reputation was set, and it has since ranked consistently among the world's top courses.

Although evidence suggests that golf was played in Dornoch as early as 1616, the club wasn't formed until 1877 when Old Tom Morris laid out nine holes, adding nine more a decade after that. Over time the layout has been tweaked and improved, most notably by Dornoch native Donald Ross, who began his career as a greenkeeper here before going on to design more than 400 courses in America.

Few links are blessed with a more dramatic location, stretched along the north shore of the Dornoch Firth. The first two holes offer little hint at the scenic splendour to come, but number two does give a taste of the challenge, playing 184 yards to a table top green with steep, deep falloffs on both sides. Miss this putting surface and you had best channel the spirit of Phil Mickelson if you want to save par.

It is at the third tee that the full glory of the course unfolds, a vast amphitheatre of linksland embraced by an enormous gorse-covered hill on the left with a swath of sandy beach and the shimmering firth to the right. This is a glorious place to play golf.

The next three holes—par fours all—play along the base of the gorse-clad hill, their fairways pitching from left to right en route to enormous plateau greens that are guarded by bunkers. But they also protect themselves with an assortment of contours, swales, runoffs, and fallaways.

At number six it's another testing par three, nestled exquisitely into the big hillside with bunkers left and an evil abyss to the right. If there is a weakness to the course it is the next two holes, which were part of a 1946 renovation after a World War II airbase appropri-

◄ An aerial view of Royal Dornoch, with the par three 6th green at the bottom of the picture, and, just above it, the 12th and 5th greens.

ated the land that had been used for the last six holes. A steeply uphill walk of 150 yards transports us from the splendour below to more pasture-like terrain for the long, flat, straight seventh while number eight presents one of the few blind shots, a drive into the clouds that tumbles toward a punchbowl green, a blessed return to true linksland.

This is the farthest reach of the course and the road back is a strong one, beginning with the first of only two par fives, stretching 529 yards along the edge of the sea. At little number 11, you can sometimes feel the ocean spray as you try to make the ball sit on a narrow, two-tiered green surrounded by bunkers and dips. Into the wind, these 174 yards can be a fairway wood or driver but downwind keeping the ball on the green is extremely difficult.

After another charmer of a par three—surrounded by no fewer than seven bunkers—comes the centre-piece of the homeward stretch, the 14th hole known as foxy, a 445-yard par four that Harry Vardon called "the most natural hole in golf." There is not a bunker in sight but on the right side a series of tall ridges jut like immense fingers into the line of play advising a tee shot that bends left-ward to avoid them. However, even the best drive leaves a tall assignment into an extremely narrow green that rises six feet above fairway. This is a green that can be hit in

only two ways—with a well judged, crisply struck shot or with a lucky miss that clambers up the slope and comes to rest before running off the back.

There is a story of a club member who once aced the 13th and followed with a birdie on 14. Back in the clubhouse, one of his fellow members said to him "I can understand how you aced the 13th, but how in hell did you get a 3 on Foxy?"

Number 16 returns uphill to the clubhouse—for Dornoch members playing a friendly match that has been closed out, this often signals an early visit to the 19th hole. Otherwise it's back down the hill to a diagonally sloping fairway that climbs back to a plateau green. The finishing hole is a brute—456 yards uphill and left to right with bunkers and gorse to be dealt with. A gully just in front of the green complicates the approach.

Those who three-putt this hole are advised not to skulk to the clubhouse with their heads down, as the path crosses directly in front of the first tee.

To be in Dornoch in the warmth of early summer, when the fragrant gorse is in its full golden bloom is to experience something unique and sublime. The British Amateur has twice been played here and it will surely return, as will the thousands of golfers who have dis-covered that splendidly isolated beauty is well worth the trip.

Royal Dornoch ⤖ № 10

The tabletop 10th green, bunkered to the front and left, has a small ridge through the middle and falls off steeply to the right and back.

Royal Dornoch 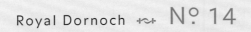 Nº 14

No 14, Foxy by name and nature. The approach will need to be either superb or extremely lucky if the green is to be its final resting place.

Royal Dornoch ↬ № 18

Dornoch's subtle challenge persists straight
through to the 18th green, with a Valley of Sin
to the front, a fall-off to the right and bunkers
strategically placed.

ROYAL TROON

Six hundred yards from the ninth tee at Prestwick is the ninth green—at Royal Troon. The two courses couldn't be closer geographically, or more removed in personality.

Prestwick is your little old aunt—well past her prime but a twinkle in her eye. Eccentric, unpredictable, and possessed of a maddening ability to find you out, she's nonetheless a hoot to be around. Troon is her younger sister—the one who never got married—dour, strait-laced and generally unappreciated. She warms up occasionally but never loses her austere mien. Take liberties with her and you'll suffer.

Troon, which held its first Open Championship in 1923—two years before Prestwick held its last—is a classic links with nine holes out and nine back, all spread across a rippling landscape dotted with grassy sandhills and deep, steep-faced bunkers.

The first six holes run straight southward along the edge of the Firth of Clyde, with splendid views of the Isle of Arran, the Mull of Kintyre, and in the distance, the rocky loaf known as Ailsa Craig. Sadly, the golf itself over this opening third of the course is less than exhilarating—three short, flat and relatively similar par fours start things off, and they're followed by two par fives sandwiching a three. The standout hole is six, a par five that winds 599 narrow yards to a green squeezed into the dunes.

Thereafter, the route turns inland for the most compelling stretch of the course; six holes that bend and bob through surging sandhills. One of the game's most famous holes comes at the little par-3 8th known as the Postage Stamp. The shortest hole in Open Championship golf, it plays 123 yards to a sliver of a green set in a hillside and surrounded by deep bunkers. It was here in the 1973 Open that 72-year-old Gene Sarazen, making a ceremonial appearance on the 50th anniversary of his last Troon Open, scored a hole-in-one. The next day on the same hole he caught a bunker then holed out for a two. Most stories here are less inspiring—in 1997 Tiger Woods took a 6 and in 1950 German amateur Herman Tissies notched an inglorious 15.

The consensus toughest hole is number 11, 417 yards of scandalously narrow fairway with thick gorse, heather, and fescue on the left and a railway running along the right. Arnold Palmer once described it as the most dangerous hole he'd ever seen, despite—or perhaps because of—the fact that in winning the 1962 Open, when the hole was a par five, he played it in five under par.

The final movement of this symphony in three parts begins when the path turns north for the closing six holes. Like the opening six, they lack the character of the middle holes, but they are undeniably difficult, especially when played into the prevailing headwind. All six are tightly bunkered, a burn comes into play at the par-five 16th, and at the home hole the stone clubhouse sits just a few feet beyond the green—perhaps the lone distinction that Royal Troon shares with Prestwick.

Royal Troon ↬ Nº 8

The Postage Stamp—diabolically bunkered
and exposed to the wind, it is yard-for-yard
one of the most perilous holes in golf.

If in the process of playing the Old Course at St Andrews you should have the misfortune to dead push your tee shot at the second hole, or power slice it at the sixth, or duck hook it at the eighth, the result won't be a disaster at all, for you will find yourself standing on what, in the minds of many, is an even better test of golf— the New Course.

There is nothing new about it. Designed by Old Tom Morris in 1895, the New has been around longer than automobiles or lightbulbs or sliced bread, and not much about it has changed since its debut.

Despite being side-by-side with the Old Course and spread across the same rolling linksland, the New is a breed apart, with narrower fairways and smaller greens. Only two holes—the 3rd and 15th—share a green and in contrast to the Old where there are just two par threes and two par fives, the New serves up four threes and three fives for a total par of 71.

With less room to manoeuver, strategic options on each hole are fewer—thick stands of gorse see to that (Among St Andrews regulars the New is thought to play two to three strokes harder than its older sibling, even more in a wind). Its opening holes however, are gentle—two par fours averaging 350 yards followed by an expansive, softly-bending par five of 511 yards. Downwind, birdies can be expected.

The plot thickens at number four, a taut little dogleg where both the distance and direction must be controlled—too far left, right, or forward and the teeshot will find fescue, gorse, heather or sand. Nothing is easy about the 445-yard sixth, either. Not the drive, which must find a fast-running fairway between sidelines of heather and gorse, not the lengthy and all but blind approach, and not the sloping green, surrounded by swales and backed by more gorse. Introduce a wind and all that evil multiplies.

The heart of the challenge comes in three holes at the farthest point of this out-and-back design, beginning with the par-five 8th, 481 yards to a green hidden in a saddle fronted by twin 20-foot-high sandhills. To watch one's approach sail or bound between those monsters and onto the putting surface is one of golf's pleasures.

No par three in all of St Andrews is more daunting than number nine, 225 perilous yards along the edge of the Eden estuary to a small amphitheatre green. The back nine then begins with what may be the best hole on the course, a 464-yard par four that plays down a narrow, canted fairway that bottlenecks as it reaches a sunken green.

The back nine, despite its par of 35, is more than 300 yards longer than the front, thanks to a brutish last three holes. Number 16, the number-one stroke hole,

◄ The approach to number 4, one of several testing par fours.

plays 431 yards, often into the wind, to a green whose right-hand entrance is blocked by a deep bunker. Similarly, two deep pots stare back from the right side of the 17th, discouraging anyone who aspires to draw a ball onto this par three of 225 yards.

The home hole, heading back to the St Andrews Links Clubhouse (which opened exactly 100 years after the course) seems straightforward enough until you realize that any approach that rolls a half dozen or so paces beyond the green will find itself at the starter's window, thoroughly out-of-bounds. This is one place where the best advice on the approach shot is to take one less club than you think you need.

St Andrews New ⇄ № 10

The semi-blind 10th, possibly the best hole on the course. At 445 yards, it requires two strong, accurate shots.

St Andrews New ⚏ № 16

Number 16, stroke index one, plays 430 yards into the prevailing wind. The green is protected by two pot bunkers to the right side.

The nine courses on which the Open Championship currently rotates are for the most part ancient venues. The Old Course dates back more than half a millennium and seven others are each at least a century old. There is, however, one exception: Turnberry. Although golf has been played on this land for more than a hundred years, the Ailsa Course at Turnberry did not make her debut until 1951. She reigns as a glowing princess among dowager queens, far younger and prettier than them all.

Turnberry is often referred to as the "Pebble Beach of Scotland", partly because the name refers not simply to a golf course but to a world-recognized resort—a rare championship venue open to the public 365 days a year—but also because of the magnificence of her setting, beside a rocky shoreline overlooking the sea. Just as no championship course in America comes closer to the ocean than Pebble Beach, no championship course in Great Britain comes closer than Turnberry.

The similarities extend to the routing and rhythm of the courses as well. Pebble is often faulted for its lacklustre early holes and the same may be said of Turnberry, which opens with three parallel par fours that head tamely up and back on relatively featureless terrain. As at Pebble, however, hole number four signals the start of a stretch of seaside holes, stunning for both their challenge and their beauty.

Number four, a 165-yard par three, plays to a small plateau green niched into sandhills. Wind can wreak havoc here as a miss to the left will sail toward the beach and anything short and right will tumble into a massive bunker at the base of a hill.

The picturesque Turnberry lighthouse comes into view at the tee of number five, but this superbly natural par four is what commands one's attention. Bending 442 yards right to left through a broad corridor formed by two dune ridges, it culminates in a slim, tightly bunkered green framed exquisitely by sandhills.

Holes six and seven are larger replicas of four and five, number six playing 231 all-carry yards from one perch in the hills to another. Into a stiff wind, it's all but unreachable, while the massive bunker on the fronting hillside is all too easy to find.

Number seven plays true to its name (Roon the Ben), arcing through a gauntlet of six bunkers and then uphill to a relatively open green. At 538 yards from the championship tee it can be an easy par five for the pros, but from the regular men's tees of 475 yards, it's the hardest par four on the course.

The scenic highlight of Turnberry—and arguably the scenic highlight of Scottish links golf—comes at the championship tee of the ninth hole, set out on a tiny rock perch above the sea, with jaw-dropping views of the Firth of Clyde and turtle-backed Ailsa Craig. Just to the left is the Turnberry Lighthouse and the remains of Turnberry Castle, birthplace of Scotland's King Robert the Bruce. And straight ahead is a 200-yard carry to a

◀ Few courses enjoy a more idyllic setting than Turnberry.

narrow hogback fairway leading 452 yards to an angled green surrounded by mounds and hollows. There is not a bunker on the hole, but none is needed.

Nowhere are the waters of the firth more in play than at the 10th, which winds leftward around a rocky cove. But even straight shots are imperilled at this par four, first by a pair of pot bunkers in the drive zone and then by an island bunker fifty yards short of the green—a hazard that comes very much into play in a headwind and comes into mind regardless of the conditions.

The last of the seaside holes is number 11, playing 175 yards to a green flanked by bunkers, the deep one on the left posing the greater peril. Then the course winds inward and upward through a trio of par fours, the first of them playing beside an abandoned airstrip on the left and a monument on a hilltop to the right, both reminders of the lives lost during the wartime years when this land was used as an RAF outpost.

The sternest one-two punch on the course is 15 and 16. Three bunkers guard the left side of the green at the par three 15th, but it is to the right that the real punishment lurks: any ball that misses the green will drop 40 feet onto the eighth fairway.

The only time that water crosses a Turnberry fairway is at the par-four 16th where a deep ravine winds

in front and to the right of the green, home to Wilson's Burn. The hole was lengthened markedly for the 2009 Open and now plays 455 yards from the back tees, making this approach the most daunting shot on the course.

No such intimidation prevails at 17, a shortish par-five, and at 18 the most distinguishing feature is the orange-roofed Turnberry Hotel, perched on a hill 300 yards beyond the green.

The 18th hole was recently renamed Duel in the Sun in honour of the first Open played here in 1977 when Tom Watson and Jack Nicklaus battled head to head the last two days, outpacing their nearest competitor by 10 strokes. At the 72nd hole, after Nicklaus recovered from the rough and then sank a miraculous 40-footer for birdie, Watson matched him with a three-footer to win the title by one shot. Thirty-two years later, Watson returned to Turnberrry at the age of 59 and thrilled the sports world by leading the championship for four days. This time he came to the home hole needing a par to score the most inspirational of victories, but tragically he suffered a bogey and then lost in a playoff to Stewart Cink.

The game giveth and the game taketh away. If there is a consolation for Watson, or for any of us who should ever suffer disappointment at Turnberry, it is this: there is no more glorious links on which to suffer.

The all-carry
230-yard 6th

A magnificent horseshoe: from right to left,
the 10th, 11th and 12th holes.

Turnberry ⌁ № 10

Number ten plays beside the sea, but it's the large bunker—with an island of turf at its centre—that attracts both attention and golf balls.

In calm conditions the 15th is a straightforward 200-yard par 3. In a wind, however, bunkers, rough and a steep fall-off to the right come demonically into play.

The 18th green sits hard by the clubhouse,
with the iconic Turnberry Hotel perched above.

View from the tee of the par four 5th,
with the 6th and 7th beyond.

TRUMP INTERNATIONAL GOLF LINKS

Opening July 2012

Trump International Golf Links ⌇ Nº 18

The bunker strewn 18th with 18 bunkers in view